Sunset

make it your own : **Baths**

By Jeanne Huber and the Editors of *Sunset*

Contents

Sunset

©2012 by Time Home Entertainment Inc.
135 West 50th Street, New York, NY 10020

ISBN-10: 0-376-01636-1   ISBN-13: 978-0-376-01636-2
Library of Congress Control Number: 2012932450
First printing 2012. Printed in the United States of America.

OXMOOR HOUSE
VP, PUBLISHING DIRECTOR: Jim Childs
CREATIVE DIRECTOR: Felicity Keane
BRAND MANAGER: Fonda Hitchcock
MANAGING EDITOR: Rebecca Benton

SUNSET PUBLISHING
PRESIDENT: Barb Newton
VP, EDITOR-IN-CHIEF: Kitty Morgan
CREATIVE DIRECTOR: Mia Daminato

CONTRIBUTORS TO THIS BOOK
AUTHOR: Jeanne Huber
MANAGING EDITOR: Karen Macklin
SERIES EDITOR: Anna Nordberg
ART DIRECTOR: Andrew Faulkner
PHOTO EDITOR: Philippine Scali
PRODUCTION MANAGER: Linda M. Bouchard
PROJECT EDITOR: Sarah H. Doss
COPY EDITOR: Barbara Feller-Roth
PHOTO COORDINATOR: Danielle Johnson
TECHNICAL ADVISER: Scott Gibson
SENIOR IMAGING SPECIALIST: Kimberley Navabpour
PROOFREADER: Lesley Bruynesteyn
INDEXER: Marjorie Joy

FRONT COVER PHOTO: The projects in this book inspired this creative display. We painted the room based on the instructions on page 56, and painted the window trim based on the instructions on page 62. Then we created the faux Roman shades by slightly adapting the instructions on page 120.

To order additional publications, call **1-800-765-6400**
For more books to enrich your life, visit **oxmoorhouse.com**
Visit Sunset online at **sunset.com**
For the most comprehensive selection of Sunset books, visit **sunsetbooks.com**

IMPORTANT SAFETY WARNING—PLEASE READ

Introduction

At *Sunset*, we love to reinvent spaces, especially practical ones. Enter the bathroom. People often think of this as the most utilitarian room in the house, the place where you shower or brush your teeth. This room also has to provide storage for items small and large. But that doesn't mean they can't be beautiful. In fact, when you consider the amount of time that you spend in your bath, it might be the room that's crying out for a makeover the most.

In this book, you'll find projects on how to make any bathroom more stylish, inviting, and, yes, practical. You will learn how to transform an entire space with an expert paint job, create new storage, build mirrors and shelving, and paint stencils onto cabinets, shades, and tubs. We'll also show you how to turn an old hutch into a practical storage unit, paint your toilet seat with a playful design, etch star shapes into your vanity cabinet, and create a wall of photos above the bath, just for fun. Want to paint stripes? Repaint your claw-foot tub? Yep, we can show you how to do that, too.

Sure, it might seem easier to call in the contractors or painters, but it'll cost you a bundle—and the process will be a lot less rewarding. There's nothing quite like finishing a project, then stepping back to see the beauty you've created. And the best part: You get to see your masterpiece every day because it's now a part of your home!

The projects in this book range in the amount of time and expertise they take—and that will vary depending on where your skills lie (like whether you're better with a hammer or a sewing needle). Start with something within your comfort zone and then expand from there. We know how rewarding it is to design your home to be exactly the way you want it, and we hope this book will help you create a bath you love.

The Editors

1

Find your style

A well-designed bathroom makes your home instantly more inviting. The good news is, there are simple changes you can make to your bathroom in a weekend, or even a few hours, that can take it from just utilitarian to stylish and serene.

Find Your Style

It's true: A bathroom must be functional. But that doesn't mean it can't also be beautiful. Your bathroom is often the first place you see in the morning, when you take your shower before work, and the last place you see at night when you brush your teeth before bed. Like every other room in your home, you want your bathroom to be comfortable and inviting!

Selecting a style for your bathroom is like selecting a style for any room in the home. You begin with broad themes and palettes, and branch out from there. To get you started, here are some examples of traditional home design styles.

If you have multiple bathrooms, they can reflect different styles—one could be Romantic, and the other could be Natural and Earthy. And any of your bathrooms can mix and match styles. Romantic Boho and Playful? Why not!

For extra fun, come up with an original name for your style, such as Natural Chic or Cozy Boho. This is a great way to pinpoint the look you want, and it will help you stay true to your vision when choosing paint, tile, accessories, and fixtures.

Quick Tip: Take Risks

Paint is not permanent—that's why it's the most favored interior design tool. So go with that bold color palette you've been dreaming about! You can always repaint later if your tastes change.

Clean and Modern
Soothing wall colors with crisp trim details—perfect if you like the feeling of being in a spa. Add well-spaced towel hooks (page 114). Blues, whites, grays, yellows.

Cozy
Neutral colors and a comforting design that consists of practical details, like a painted stool or a refinished tea cart (page 94). Warm whites, neutrals, pale blues and greens, yellows.

Romantic

A lavish use of warm colors, decorative lighting, and soft details like a floral sink skirt (page 95). Pinks, blush, grays, soft whites.

Boho

Vibrant colors and bohemian touches, such as a single tile displayed as art, clipboards for storage (see page 128), or fabric pennants (page 138). Greens, yellows, blues, purples.

Natural and Earthy

Wood or other nature-inspired details, like the floating box shelves on page 88 and the wood knob towel hooks on page 114. Warm whites, beige, greens, browns.

Fun and Playful

Bright colors and bold design choices, such as an accent wall (page 64), a striped floor (page 72) or a painted toilet seat (page 152). Bright yellows, oranges, pinks, blues.

First, Be Practical

When updating your bath, you'll encounter issues you don't have with other rooms. Baths are small, get damp easily from shower mist, need more privacy than other rooms, and require good ventilation and smart storage options. These are all things to consider when choosing paint colors, fixtures, accessories, or fabric. For instance, you might love sheer fabrics, but that doesn't mean they are the best choice to cover a bathroom window that looks onto a street. And though matte might be your favorite paint finish, it's harder to clean than glossier finishes, so isn't the best choice for a moist bathroom. As you create visions for each of your bathrooms, take the following into consideration.

What Kind of Bathroom Do You Have?

Half bath (powder room). A half bath, also known as a powder room, has a sink but no shower or tub. It's often small and cozy. While its tight quarters can make it feel a little short on storage space, updating a half bath has a plus: The minimal amount of square footage means that you will be able to afford higher-priced materials. For example, if there is an expensive wallpaper that you just adore, you could simply paper one wall (perhaps the one behind the mirror and sink) for impact. These spaces also give you an opportunity to take chances. Bold colors often work well in small spaces, creating a jewel-box effect. Consider painting the ceiling a glossy cobalt, for example, and then hanging a chandelier to make the room sparkle.

Shared bath. When there is only one full bathroom in a house, it is usually a high-traffic area that needs to function well for everyone. Consider adding hooks and extra towel racks, shelves above the toilet, and practical open storage (countertop jars and baskets). Since space is at a premium, think about using paint colors and vibrant linens to express your style instead of decorative hampers or bulky magazine racks.

Shared bath with kids. Choose materials that are tough enough to withstand a lot of use—and are safe and easy to clean. This probably isn't the best place for a lace shower curtain, even if you love a romantic style. There are lots of ways to make a kids' bath appealing to you, too. Removable wall decals are a great way to add personality. So are brightly colored towels, patterned shower curtains, and fun bath mats.

Master bath. A master bathroom is a private oasis. It often has space enough for two sinks, and separate shower and bath areas. Since it's all yours, make it a relaxing, inviting place. Easy touches like candles (see the candle ledges on page 112), a dimmer switch, and a music system go a long way to making the space soothing and enjoyable.

Is There Natural Lighting?

A room's natural lighting should be considered when you select colors. A room with a lot of natural light can handle strong colors, whereas a room that relies on overhead lighting works best with more subdued colors. For instance, you may be dreaming of deep purple for your walls, but if the natural light in the room is low, skip it. The effect will be more dungeon-like than dreamy.

Some half baths don't have a window; in those cases, make sure you have ample artificial lighting that is also not harsh. If a room is very small, consider multiple small light sources. These can add dimension to the room, making it appear larger, and decrease a glaring effect that one bold overhead fixture might have. For example, sconces flanking the vanity mirror plus a soft overhead light can help make a windowless half bath more inviting.

The vanity mirror is the most important spot to light properly. This is where people will be fixing their hair, shaving, et cetera, so the light should be as even and natural as possible. Wiring the lighting fixtures so that they are controlled by dimmer switches allows for lots of flexibility so that the light can be bright when needed, and be low and more flattering at other times.

What's the Size of the Bathroom?

Does the room feel too big, too small, or just right? Color and design can change the perception of volume. If the room is small, consider painting the ceiling a light blue or decorating with framed mirrors (page 144) for a more spacious effect. If a room feels too big, use standing storage (see the refinished hutch on page 100) and rich colors to make it feel cozier. Also, consider installing a pendant light fixture. For some examples of how to make a small space feel bigger, see page 14.

What's Already There?

You may not have the time or the budget to *completely* revamp your bathroom(s)—most people don't. As you develop a vision for each bathroom you want to restyle, note what can go, what needs to stay, and how to best work with all of it.

Collect Inspiration

You know those pretty style boards that designers put together with photos and color swatches? Well, you can make one yourself! It will help you understand your own preferences for style and color.

To create a style board, buy a corkboard and some tacks from a local art supply store. (Or do a more basic version with a big piece of cardboard and tape, or simply collect images in a file or binder.) Fill your style board with magazine pages, photos of rooms that inspire you, colors you love, or vacation photos that evoke a mood you want to re-create. Hotel spas are a great place for design inspiration. You can also add paint swatches or fabric samples to the board. The more elements you assemble, the more you'll have to choose from in the end. Tack things up and take things down as you play with the look, and watch your style unfold. And don't despair if your ideas don't seem to blend. This is the stage to go with your gut and experiment!

Once your style board is full of ideas, it's time to take stock. Look at everything and see if there are colors or styles that keep showing up. Discard the outliers or anything that you don't really love. Leave the board up on a wall in your house for a while and take note of what keeps drawing your eye. Eventually, you'll know which direction you want to go. Be patient—sometimes it takes a little while before you land on a style you love.

Quick Tip: Sheer or Opaque Fabric?

Sheer fabrics are good for filtering light through windows and providing some privacy, but only when it's lighter outside than it is indoors. At night, you'll need a more opaque window covering, such as a roll-down shade behind the sheer curtain, or an opaque drape in front of it.

Select Your Paint Colors

There are many factors to consider when choosing colors for your bath.

Colors and Mood

Style experts say that color can impact your mood. Here are some common color-mood combinations.

Of course, everyone reacts differently to colors. Feel free to deviate from the guidelines to match your own preferences and personality, especially in rooms that won't see a lot of company, such as bedrooms and private bathrooms.

Use Color to Add Volume

Small bathrooms present common problems for homeowners and renters alike because they have limited space and can feel stuffy and claustrophobic. But color and style go miles toward making a small powder room seem roomy. Here are some effective techniques.

Use light colors. Light colors, including white, brighten and reflect light, whereas dark colors absorb light and make a room feel smaller.

Use a bold, dark color with lots of glass and mirror accents. These accents reflect light, making the space seem larger even though it's painted with a dark color. (For mirror ideas, check out pages 98, 118, 122, 126, and 144.)

Quick Tip: Beware of Glare

Some whites are much brighter than others and therefore reflect more light. If a room is flooded with natural light, very bright white paint can make the space seem blinding. For naturally bright rooms, choose a white with warm undertones.

Paint one wall a deep, rich color, such as cobalt blue or magenta. This can change the apparent depth of a room. A far wall painted in a dark color tends to extend the gaze, making the space seem to go on forever. (Check out the accent wall on page 64.)

Paint the ceiling the same color as the walls. This creates a cohesive feeling by avoiding a visual line break between the two surfaces.

Steer clear of dusky or muted shades. These make a room look smaller. Clean colors, no matter what the shade, work best.

Choose the Right White

White is wonderful as an accent or trim color, and as a main color. When used as an accent or trim color (page 60), it can bring the main colors into sharp relief. When used as a main color, it can provide a crisp, clean backdrop for a room—think art gallery—that lets architecture, cabinets, and accessories take the spotlight.

But all whites are not created equal. They can be divided into two categories: warm and cool. Warm whites have yellow, red, or brown undertones; cool whites have tints of greens and blues. When choosing whites, be sure to try a few samples in your existing space. Some whites make certain furniture or fabrics look dirty, whereas other whites make colors sing. Experiment with different whites to gauge which ones work best.

Create Tints and Shades

You can change colors to make them lighter or darker by adding white or black to the mix. To create a new tint, add white to the paint color; to create a new shade, add black. If the new color is one you'll need to replicate, you may want to keep track of the exact amounts of white or black you added to the original color.

Choose Flattering Hues

Some colors are more flattering than others—an important factor to consider in a room where people spend a lot of time looking in the mirror. For instance, green may be your favorite color, but the wrong green can make you look like you just got home from a rough journey at sea. Choose colors—and lighting—that make people look good.

» Consider the same color principles when choosing tile, cabinets, and accessories.

Quick Tip: Collect Paint Chips

Paint chips can help you narrow down your choices, so collect a lot of them and tape them up on a bathroom wall at home to see what you like best. When you go to the paint store, bring clippings from your style board, as well as photos of features you aren't changing in the room (like tile) to help you make your paint chip selections.

Test Your Colors

So you've got your style and color palettes all set. Now it's time to paint, right? Well, not quite yet. Number one painting mistake: Not testing your colors before painting the entire room! There is nothing worse than finishing a bathroom, only to realize that the color is just plain wrong.

The solution: Test your paint. Paint chips are famously just a little bit off, so use actual paint. Lots of paint and hardware stores offer inexpensive sample-size containers so that you can test a few colors on your wall before committing. Purchase a few samples and brush them on the wall (at least one square foot per color). Paint a few colors side by side so that you can compare. Let the paint dry, and then take a step back and consider: Does the color look good only in the morning when the light is soft? Did the paint dry darker than expected? Continue testing colors until you find the right one.

Get Creative with Storage, Accessories, and Art

Bathrooms present unusual design challenges because they're typically small but need to provide ample storage space. But storage solutions can be fun, decorative, and creative. In this book you'll learn that storage opportunities exist all over the bathroom—on the walls, under the sink, in the shower, on shelves, and behind doors.

Mirrors are a particularly important feature in a bathroom, since you use them constantly. One well-lit mirror placed above the sink is sufficient for most bathrooms, but multiple mirrors can be a nice touch if you have the wall space. Mirrors are an especially effective way to make a small bathroom feel larger. If you have the opportunity to install a full-wall mirror, do it. For style *and* function, you can even display a series of framed mirrors (see page 144).

And remember: Not everything in the bathroom has to be functional. Sometimes small, artful touches can give a huge boost to the ambience. Consider framed prints, stencils, decorative tiles or glass, fabric pennants, wallpaper touches, and anything else that adds color and style. Just make sure that it is resistant to damp conditions! See Chapter 6 for some starter ideas.

Quick Tip: Fixing a Color
If you bring paint home and discover that the color you thought you wanted doesn't look quite right, go back to the paint store and see if they can add more pigment or more white to fix it.

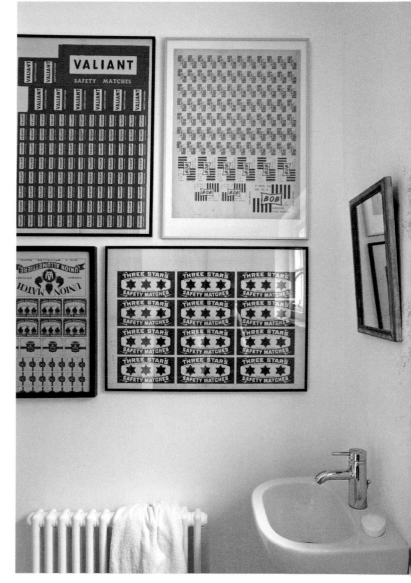

These framed matchbox covers add color, style, and personality to a simple white bathroom.

Quick Tip: Mixing Patterns
Want to combine a floral print and stripes in a room? Fabric manufacturers create mixed patterns that go well together, and they are often displayed near one another in fabric stores.

Accent Your Bathroom with Wallpaper and Fabric

You don't have to wallpaper the entire bathroom to make a statement. Bold, graphic, and sweet patterns all work well on an accent wall (page 64) or on cabinet door panels (page 76). Fabric is also ideal for creating accents in a bathroom, whether it's used as a sink skirt (page 95) or Roman shades (page 120). High-end fabrics can cost more than your mortgage payment or rent, so shop at discount fabric sources online, or browse the sale racks at fabric stores.

How to Choose Patterns and Colors for Wallpaper and Fabric

Want to give a room more impact? Wallpaper and fabric are an excellent way to do that. Here are a few things to consider.

Bold or neutral pattern. This choice often depends on how you are using the fabric or wallpaper. If you're tackling a small accent project, go for something bold and bright—after all, you want an accent. But if you are investing a lot of money and time in window coverings, you might want to choose something more adaptable, such as a delicate pattern or an interesting texture.

Bright or neutral colors. Depending on the color you choose, you can make your window curtains assume center stage or feel more like background pieces. For instance, a window dressed with a bright fabric will stand out more than one dressed with brown or tan fabric.

Vertical elements. With fabric and wallpaper, you have a choice of running the stripes or stripelike patterns horizontally or vertically, so you can make a wall or a window look wider or higher depending on how you orient the wallpaper or curtain fabric. Stripes and other strong patterns that run up and down can make ceilings look higher.

Strong geometric or floral patterns. Bold patterns like the one on the opposite page can liven up an otherwise lackluster space. Consider bold patterns for accent walls so they don't overwhelm the room.

Multiple patterns. Avoid using too many bold patterns in a room, especially if the room is small. Patterns made up of small, repeating elements aren't as risky because they often read simply as texture.

Test Your Wallpaper and Fabric

Wallpaper is often even more of a financial investment than paint, so make sure you test the pattern before you buy the whole amount for the project. Many stores and online retailers sell samples that you can place next to your tile or cabinetry to see how the colors relate. Of course, you can't preview what a pattern will look like on an entire wall, so consider getting a second opinion from a design-savvy friend.

It's equally useful to test any fabric you might be using for a sink skirt (page 95), curtain doors on a vanity (page 92), or any other projects in your bathroom. Even if you're not using very much, see how a sample of the fabric looks in the room alongside the paint colors, tile patterns, and cabinets before you invest in the needed yardage.

Finally, Be Your Own Unique Self

Designing your home is about designing a place for you to express yourself and feel comfortable and happy, and your bathroom plays a big role in that. Although it's helpful to research what professional designers and stylists suggest, ultimately your opinion is what counts. Remember: If you love it, it can't be wrong. When in doubt, *Sunset* is a fabulous resource. Visit sunset.com for endless ideas and inspiration for creating a bathroom you'll love.

Quick Tip: Keep It Dry

Wallpaper works best in a bathroom that doesn't have a lot of humidity, such as a powder room. If you want to try wallpaper in a bath that has a shower or a tub, make sure that the room has a window or a fan.

2

Getting Started

Before you start painting, sawing, sewing, and stenciling your heart out, take a few minutes to read this chapter and educate (or re-educate) yourself on how to prepare for working on your bathroom, what materials to use, and what practices are best. A little background knowledge goes a long way toward making your bathroom projects easier, safer, and more cost-efficient.

Bathroom Planning

When you update or remodel any room in the house, you have to take certain logistical things into consideration before beginning—like building codes and industry standards. Even though a full-scale remodeling is beyond the scope of this book, it will still be helpful to understand what the parameters are so you don't inadvertently change something that could cause problems later.

For example, you might decide to install the floating box shelves on page 88 directly alongside the toilet, without knowing that clear space needs to be left on both sides of a toilet. (Plumbers need clear spaces on both sides to repair or replace a toilet, so if you cramp the space, you could find yourself scrambling to take down the shelves as you're dealing with a plumbing emergency.)

Recommended Clearances

These are general guidelines. Always check with your local building department, as local rules vary.

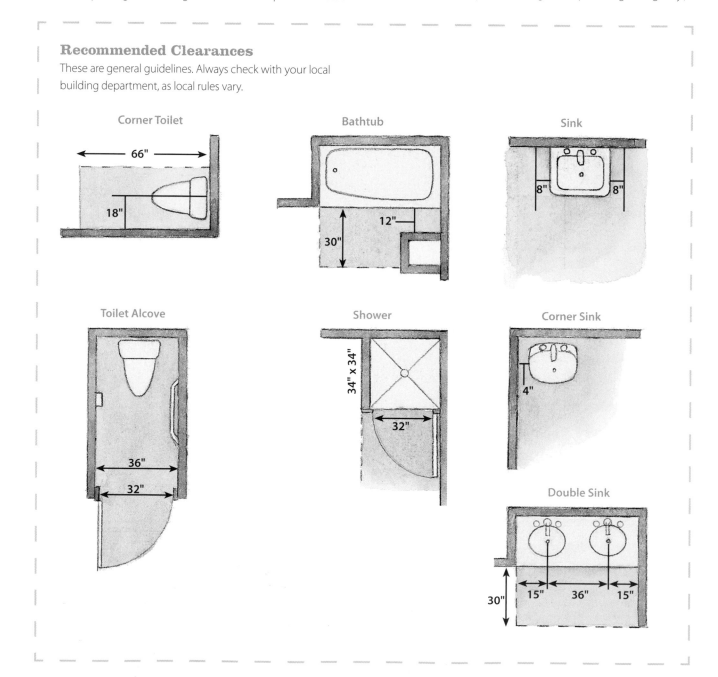

Corner Toilet — 66", 18"

Bathtub — 12", 30"

Sink — 8", 8"

Toilet Alcove — 36", 32"

Shower — 34" x 34", 32"

Corner Sink — 4"

Double Sink — 15", 36", 15", 30"

Quick Tip: Maintenance Matters

A constant drip from a leaky pipe under the sink will eventually ruin the vanity or maybe even the floor underneath. Fix any leaks as soon as you notice them to keep your bathroom in good condition. If you don't know how, call a plumber and watch as the repair is done. You might learn enough so you can do it yourself the next time.

Get to Know Paint

If you want to change the whole look of a bathroom without spending too much money or time, nothing beats a fresh coat of paint. Paint is more than simply color in a can. It's a complex compound that has three main components:

Solvent. The base of the paint that makes the paint easy to spread and then evaporates. (In water-based paint, the main solvent is water; in oil-based paint, it's mostly paint thinner.)

Pigment. The element in paint that provides the color.

Resin. The "glue" that holds the paint ingredients together and enables the paint to adhere to the wall or other surface.

Different Paints

Not all paints are created alike, so you should know what's what when it comes to types of paint. Here's a cheat sheet.

Latex paint. This water-based paint is typically used on walls, ceilings, and woodwork. It's often called acrylic paint because acrylic is commonly used as the resin. (Ironically, latex paint doesn't contain true latex, which is the milky sap of rubber trees.) Latex paint can be tinted to almost any color and is used for the majority of paint projects in this book.

Latex enamel. This water-based paint is used for hard-wearing surfaces such as woodwork and cabinets, especially in bathrooms (and kitchens). Latex enamel contains a higher percentage of resin than does standard paint, which makes it dry into a harder, tougher film. It's sold in bright, factory-formulated colors as well as in formulas that allow tinting. Use latex enamel in places that get dirty easily because it stands up to scrubbing better than latex paint.

Latex porch and floor paint. This water-based paint is made specifically for use on floors. It contains even more resin than does latex enamel, and the resin is formulated to be especially hard and scratch-resistant. Latex porch and floor paint is usually tinted at the factory, so it's available only in limited colors, but you can combine factory-made colors to create your own tints and shades.

« Available in virtually any color, latex paint is the most commonly used paint for bathroom walls.

Oil paint. This traditional type of paint combines a solvent such as paint thinner and an oil that cures into a hard finish after the solvent evaporates. Oil paint dries harder than latex and is therefore easier to wipe clean later. But we don't suggest it for any projects in this book. Why? It cracks over time, has a strong odor while it is drying, stays wet longer than water-based paint, and must be cleaned off tools with paint thinner rather than water. That said, some people do prefer it, especially for cabinets and woodwork. If you choose to substitute oil-based paint for the paints we suggest in this book, use an oil-based primer, too.

Eco-Friendly Paint

If you want to be eco-conscious, you need to take a few things into consideration when choosing the type of paint you buy. Water-based paints don't pose the fire hazard that some oil-based products do, and they release far fewer fumes as they cure. However, most water-based formulas still contain small amounts of solvents other than water, and some of these solvents can trigger allergic reactions when they are inhaled. The solvents can also dry out your skin with prolonged exposure.

For the least smelly, most environmentally friendly paints, look for low-odor products that are also low in VOCs (volatile organic compounds), preferably with certification from an independent organization such as Green Seal. Avoid products with the words "warning" or "caution" on the label or with hazardous ingredients listed on the material safety data sheet (MSDS), which the store should be able to supply.

Choose a Finish

You've chosen all your colors. You go to the store and hand the little paint chips to the person at the paint counter. And then you're asked: What kind of finish do you want? Good question. The name of a finish—such as gloss, semi-gloss, satin, eggshell, or matte—describes the amount of light that the paint reflects. But each finish has other qualities as well, and not all finishes are appropriate for all places in a bathroom. See the list below and make sure to select the right finish.

Gloss ("glossy") and semi-gloss These are the glossiest finishes you can buy, with gloss being the shiniest. These paints contain more resin than other paints, which adds shine and makes the dried paint tougher and slicker. Gloss paint is the preferred paint for trim and cabinets in a high-traffic bathroom because it's easiest to clean when it comes to mildew, oil, soap, and other bathroom messes.	**Use on:** cabinets, bathroom wood-work, and molding with undulating curves and crisp corners; also okay for bathroom walls if you want them to look shiny.	**Don't use on:** bathroom ceilings (the reflected light highlights surface imperfections and makes the ceiling seem lower).
Satin This paint has less resin and therefore less luster than gloss paint. It's still slick enough for easy cleaning in bathrooms, but the lower shine hides surface irregularities like patching over screws and nails better than gloss.	**Use on:** bathroom walls and cabinets or trim where you don't want a high-gloss look.	**Don't use on:** bathroom ceilings (for the same reasons as gloss paint), unless you want the ceiling and walls to match.
Eggshell A low-luster finish, eggshell is named for the way it resembles the slightly reflective surface of an egg. It's not ideal for most bathroom surfaces because it's harder to wipe clean, but it hides surface irregularities better than satin and gloss.	**Use on:** bathroom ceilings, and powder rooms where you want a relatively matte look but don't need to worry about oil, soap, or mildew.	**Don't use on:** other bathroom surfaces.
Matte (or flat) This paint has a somewhat rough texture (though you'd need a microscope to see it). The uneven surface causes light waves to bounce back at various angles, resulting in a surface that looks almost velvety.	**Use on:** powder room walls and ceilings where you want colors to seem especially deep and pure or want surface irregularities to blend in.	**Don't use on:** other bathroom surfaces.

« A satin finish is perfect for bathroom walls because it's easy to clean—but not too shiny.

Preparing to Paint

Painting the bathroom is easy—you just bust out the rollers and get the job done, right? Well, almost. Before you paint anything, you'll need to prepare for the job.

Plan Ahead

Excessive humidity prevents paint from curing properly. So it's best to paint your bathroom in warm, dry weather if possible, and during a time when people will be able to skip taking a shower for a day or two after you paint. If the shower must be used, ask people to keep the bathroom door open while they shower so the bathroom doesn't become steamy. The last thing you want after all your hard work is peeling paint!

Clean

In a bathroom, take it as a given that you need to wash the walls before you paint. Soap could be spattered anywhere, mildew and mold may be present, and the walls may be covered with dirt, hair, and dust. To clean walls and ceilings, use water with a few drops of household cleaner; use a liquid deglosser if the existing paint has a gloss finish. For heavier duty cleaning, you may want to use trisodium phosphate, or TSP. (It interferes with some primers, though, so check the label first.) Remove any residue from bathroom surfaces with a wallpaper sponge or a cloth, and rinse it out frequently in warm water. Allow the surface to dry before you proceed.

Patch

Before you prime and paint, fill any gouges or nail holes in the walls and trim. It's important to use patching material suitable for the surface and the type of hole. Here are some tips.

Plugging nail holes in drywall. Smear on a little lightweight spackling compound, which has the consistency of whipped cream, with a finger or a putty knife. Try to get the patch material in the holes only. If the holes are small, and if you can avoid smearing spackle on the surrounding surface, you may not need to prime the wall.

Filling dents in drywall. Use a spackle paste here because it has more body than spackling compound. Stir the paste to a creamy consistency. Then use a putty knife to press it into the dents. Apply layers no more than ¼ inch thick, or as the label recommends. Allow each layer to dry before you add the next.

Quick Tip: Apply Patch in Layers
If you're plugging a deep gouge, apply the patch material in layers. Two thin layers will dry faster than one thick layer.

Filling large holes. For this, you need something heftier, so use drywall joint compound over fiberglass mesh, which is included in hole-repair kits. Follow the instructions on the package. If the wall has a texture, complete your repair by spraying on a texture material that matches the surrounding wall's texture. If you use a spray-on texture material, first test the spray on a piece of cardboard to determine how far from the surface you must hold the can for the best result.

Patching holes in wood. Water-based wood fillers are the easiest type to use. Slightly overfill the holes, but avoid smearing filler on the surrounding area. When the patches are dry, sand them smooth with 180-grit sandpaper or a sanding sponge. Wood fillers colored to look like specific kinds of wood are helpful if you don't plan to paint afterward; these fillers, however, may not be a good choice if you *are* planning to paint because some are too waxy or oily for the paint to adhere. Check the label for the manufacturer's recommendations.

Caulking gaps. If you plan to paint the trim, it's best to caulk the gaps between the trim and the walls or the ceiling. Use latex caulk that's labeled as paintable. Cut the tip of the caulk tube with a sharp utility knife so it produces a bead the same width as the narrowest gap you want to fill. Recut the tip later for the wider gaps. Apply the caulk in a single pass along each piece of trim, then immediately smooth over it—one time only—with your finger or a dampened rag or sponge.

Dealing with Lead Paint

If you live in an older home, there's a good chance that some of the painted surfaces contain lead. In bathrooms, be especially suspicious about doors, trim, a painted wood floor, and the exterior of a claw-foot tub. Lead is toxic, and exposure to lead dust can cause serious illness, such as brain damage, especially in children. Pregnant women should also avoid exposure. Lead was banned from household paint in 1978, but people continued to use leftover paint for several years. You can easily test for lead by using a kit sold at hardware and paint stores.

If you do have lead-based paint in your home, here's what to do.

• If the paint is in good condition, simply paint over it. Try to avoid sanding it, though, as that would stir up dust and release some of the lead into your house.

• If the paint is not in good condition—and it needs to be scraped, sanded, or removed—consider having the painted surface or item replaced (if possible), or hire professionals trained in removing lead-based paint.

• If you have to scrape, sand, or remove old paint—and you suspect that it might have lead in it—always wear a NIOSH (National Institute for Occupational Safety and Health)-approved respirator to control lead exposure. And then clean up carefully with a HEPA (high-efficiency particulate-arresting) vacuum and a wet mop. Before you start, find out how to protect yourself and your family by contacting the National Lead Information Hotline at 1-800-424-LEAD, or log on to *www.epa.gov/lead*

Deglossing Your Walls

If you want to paint over gloss paint or any kind of slick unpainted surface, such as laminate, you need to create a new surface that helps the new paint to adhere. You have three options, and sometimes you may need to use a combination of these.

• Lightly sand with 180-grit sandpaper just to the point where the surface is evenly dull.

• Put on rubber gloves and wash the surface with a liquid deglosser.

• Use a primer that is formulated to adhere to slick surfaces that haven't been sanded.

Sanding is quick and doesn't require you to buy other prep products. But liquid deglosser and primer are safer options if you're dealing with lead paint (see page 29). Deglosser is better than primer when you want to preserve crisp architectural details and you don't need primer for another reason. In many cases, even if you use deglosser, it's good to sand (assuming the paint is lead-free), and this is what we recommend in the paint projects in this book. But use your own judgment. If the paint is not chipped, and the deglosser took out all of the shine, you can skip sanding.

Sand

You may also need to sand the surface before you begin painting. If the surface is rough or the paint is chipped, sanding will smooth it; if the surface is slick from glossy paint, a light sanding creates little grooves that help the new paint to adhere. (If you use deglosser or a primer made for slick surfaces, you may be able to skip sanding; see the sidebar at left.) You have two options when sanding.

Sand by hand. This is the best approach on three-dimensional surfaces such as furniture and on delicate surfaces or ones where you want only a light sanding, such as old paint that you're just trying to scuff up. On a rough surface, begin with a relatively rough grit and work in stages up through finer and finer grits. On a very rough surface, you might want to start with 80 grit, then 100, followed by 120 or 150, and finally 180. For scuffing up old paint, use only 180 grit.

Use an electric sander. When the surface is very rough or very large, machine sanding saves you a lot of time and labor. Use a palm or random-orbital sander for most pre-painting prep. A belt sander is very aggressive, so it's suitable only where the surface is very rough or you need to remove a tough existing finish (one that doesn't contain lead—see caution on page 29). With any type of sander, keep the machine in constant motion. Electric sanders stir up a lot of dust, so wear a disposable respirator, sold at most hardware stores.

Masking

With a steady hand and a lot of experience, professional painters learn to paint right up to molding or a corner without masking the adjoining surface. But for peace of mind—and neater results—it's usually better to cover adjoining surfaces before you begin. Follow these steps to ensure good results.

Use painter's masking tape. The adhesive on the back isn't as strong as the adhesive on regular masking tape, so when you remove it, it's less likely to pull off the paint underneath or leave adhesive residue behind. For most painting projects, use medium-tack tape and remove it within the number of days that the manufacturer recommends. Another option: **Edge-blocking tape.** This is a special kind of painter's masking tape formulated to absorb any paint that seeps under the edge so you wind up with a crisp paint line. It costs more but is worth using, especially for stripes or other intricate designs where touching up would take a lot of time.

Apply the tape. Unroll a workable length or cut a piece long enough for the section you want to mask. Working in short sections, align the edge of the tape that will establish the paint line, and apply the tape, pressing down firmly on the edge of the tape that faces the side where you'll be painting.

Remove the tape. Pull it off at a moderate rate. If you yank it off too fast, the tape may tear off in slivers. If you pull too slowly, you increase the chance of removing the paint underneath. Start by pulling the tape at a 45-degree angle to the surface. If that leaves adhesive residue behind, slow down and raise the angle, so that you are pulling the tape at a 90-degree angle to the wall. If the tape pulls off paint at the side, cut neatly along the side edge of the tape with a sharp utility knife.

Protect Your Floor and Fixtures

Painting a bathroom is more fun when you're not worried about ruining your tub, sink, or tile, so cover surfaces well. For many of the smaller projects in this book, you can use flattened cardboard boxes or sheets of newspaper to protect surfaces. If you need to stand inside a tub or rest ladder legs there, slip a piece of cardboard into the tub first so you don't scratch the finish. If you're painting the entire bathroom, or even just a wall, consider the following options.

Plastic drop cloths. These block spills, but they are slippery, so they are best used to cover sinks and bathtubs, not the floor.

Heavy fabric, such as canvas. This is a good option for covering the floor.

Brown paper drop cloth with a plastic layer in the middle. This is another good option for the floor.

If you use a fabric drop cloth, always use it with the same side up, and pack it away with the painted face folded in on itself. This way, any paint drips that dry on the cloth will stay there rather than coming loose and littering the floor the next time you use the cloth.

Applying painter's tape with precision will ensure clean lines.

Be sure to prime whenever you are dramatically changing the color of a wall. A tinted primer, as pictured here, is especially useful if you plan to paint a dark color.

Get Ready to Prime

Primer is an undercoat that helps paint adhere to surfaces and cover well. Primer costs less than decorative paint and can often substitute for one or two layers of decorative paint, allowing you to use fewer coats of the pricier paint. Primer also helps paint grip better to slick surfaces, which can be especially helpful in a bathroom, where finishes tend to be more glossy than in other rooms.

Primers are the supporting actors on the paint stage; they grip, hide, and seal, helping decorative paint look better. You can skip priming if you are painting over existing paint of the same type. But in most other cases, using a primer first will save you time.

Prime when you are going to:

» dramatically change the color of a surface

» cover old gloss paint

» cover old oil paint with latex paint

» paint a surface you just patched

» paint bare wood

» paint new drywall

What Type of Primer to Use

As with paint, all primers are not created alike.

Water-based primer. Use this for most projects.

Oil-based primer. Use this if you plan to use oil-based paint or for any problematic surfaces (it adheres better than water-based primer).

Shellac-based primer. Use this for priming over problematic or especially slick surfaces, such as laminate or glossy oil paint that you don't want to scuff-sand first because it might contain lead. Shellac-based primer seals especially well, so you can use it before you repaint a surface that has a water stain. Shellac-based primer is ready to re-coat in just 45 minutes, so you can get started on the decorative paint sooner.

Primer-sealer. Some manufacturers make a water-based primer called primer-sealer (or adhesion sealer), which performs nearly as well as a shellac-based primer—and smells better when drying. Primer-sealer can usually also be used as a prep product under wallcoverings; check the label to be sure.

Quick Tip: Oil Paint Test
Not sure if the old paint is oil or water based? Rub a small area with denatured alcohol on a cloth. Latex paint will rub off, but oil paint will not.

Know Your Tools

Some projects are best done with a brush, some with a roller, and some with a combination of the two.

Brushes

A brush delivers paint more precisely than a roller or a sprayer, so it's the best tool when you want to cut in paint at the edges of a room, paint the trim (page 60), or create detailed projects like those in Chapter 6. Consider the following options while choosing brushes. For standard painting, it's helpful to have brushes in different sizes, such as a small one (1 to 1½ inches wide) for details and a wider one (2 to 3 inches wide) for the main expanse.

Synthetic or natural. Use a brush with synthetic bristles for water-based paint. Natural bristles swell when damp, making painting messier when you are using water-based paint. Natural bristles are perfect for oil-based finishes, though.

Angled or straight. Angled brushes are ideal for reaching into corners—important if you're painting windows or the cubby-holes in a bookcase. Use straight brushes when you are painting wide, flat surfaces.

Quality or cheap. More expensive brushes tend to have more helpful features—such as frayed bristle tips that minimize brush marks, and spacers between rows of bristles that allow the brush to hold more paint. For most painting projects, use good brushes. However, inexpensive brushes are perfect for touch-ups because they don't hold as much paint so they are easier to rinse clean. Bristle brushes are best for touching up paint applied with a brush; foam brushes are good for roller-job touch-ups.

Long or short. In most cases, you want a brush with fairly long bristles; they hold a lot of paint and help even out the finish. However, if you're stenciling, short bristles packed into a thick bundle work better. To stencil, you don't brush across a surface, as you would when painting a wall. You dip just the tips of the brush into the finish, blot off the excess on a piece of scrap paper, and then dab the brush in and out to transfer the paint to the open areas of the stencil.

« Use the right brushes and rollers for a beautiful finish like this one.

Rollers

To paint a wall or a ceiling quickly and evenly, use a roller. Keep the following in mind while choosing a roller.

Roller cover material. With water-based paint, use a roller cover made of a synthetic material such as nylon or polyester. Mohair and lambswool rollers are for oil-based finishes only.

Nap (or pile) length. This is the thickness of the fabric on the roller head. On smooth walls, use a short-nap roller. On rough surfaces, such as heavily textured walls or fireplace brick, use a longer nap.

Width and diameter. Mini rollers, about the size of a hot dog, are ideal for painting both sides of a corner at once and for applying finish to small areas. Big, wide rollers are most efficient for painting large areas.

Roller frame (or handle). If you are painting ceilings and high walls, consider a roller frame that has screw threads on the end so you can attach an extension handle.

Other Tools You'll Need

In addition to rollers and brushes, make sure you have a ladder, paint tray(s), razor blades (for cutting tape while masking), and cleaning materials. A microfiber dust cloth works best for removing sawdust and lint because its static charge attracts the small particles. A wallpaper sponge, which is identical to a tile sponge, works better than a kitchen sponge for wiping away residue because it has small pores that pick up a lot of material and it's easy to rinse clean. Rubber gloves, like the ones you'd use for dishwashing, protect your skin from harsh cleaning agents. If you need more dexterity and are just trying to keep paint off your fingers, thin disposable gloves work better.

Understand Wallpaper

Besides using paint to transform bathroom walls, you can also use wallpaper. Take the following things into consideration.

Coated and uncoated. Most wallpaper sold in the United States these days is coated with plastic so it's easy to clean. The plastic also makes the wallpaper impervious to moisture, which is why coated wallpaper is often recommended for use in bathrooms. Polyvinyl chloride, called vinyl or PVC, is the most common plastic coating. There are other plastic coatings, as well as types that have a sheet of vinyl laminated to the surface. Uncoated, all-paper wallpaper has no plastic coating and isn't usually washable or water-resistant. It's usually not recommended for use in a bathroom.

Don't use a vinyl-coated wallpaper on an exterior wall if you live in a humid climate where you run an air conditioner. Condensation may form under the wallcovering on outside walls (because humidity gets through the wall from the exterior), and it won't evaporate because of the coating, resulting in mildew. Instead, use a breathable wallcovering that's specified for use in high-moisture environments—or stick with paint.

Unpasted and pre-pasted. Unpasted wallcovering needs wallpaper paste to adhere it to the wall. Pre-pasted wallcovering comes with adhesive on it; you just add water and wait the recommended time. Either type of wallpaper can be used for projects in this book, though in some cases one is recommended over the other.

Peelable and strippable. Peelable wallpaper has a vinyl-coated layer that can be peeled off. The paper backing, however, needs to be removed with water or wallpaper stripper. Still, it's a big improvement over non-peelable vinyl wallpaper, which is a lot more difficult to remove. Strippable wallpaper can be easily removed—just pull it off, without using any tools, chemicals, or water.

Washable and scrubbable. If a wallcovering is washable, you can wipe away smudges using mild soap, water, and a sponge or soft cloth. But you need to be relatively gentle or you could wear out the wallcovering. With a scrubbable wallcovering, you can really scrub it. If you buy wallpaper that's neither washable nor scrubbable, you can make it easier to clean by brushing or rolling on some clear matte acrylic after the wallpaper paste dries.

> **Quick Tip: Removing Unpeelable Wallpaper**
> To remove vinyl unpeelable wallpaper, pepper the paper with holes (using a wallpaper scoring tool), and then sponge or roll on wallpaper stripper, or hot water mixed with a little white vinegar. Wait for the paper to turn dark or to bubble, and then scrape it off the wall.

Know Your Tools

You need only a few specialized tools to install wallpaper. In addition to the basics listed below, make sure you have a ladder or step stool, a carpenter's level, scissors, and a razor blade.

Wallpaper water tray (for pre-pasted paper only). This long, narrow tray is perfect for submerging pre-pasted wallcoverings in order to dampen and activate the adhesive. A bathtub or a plastic storage bin also works.

Wallpaper paste brush (for unpasted paper only). This short, stout brush is designed to spread adhesive onto large unpasted pieces quickly and with minimum mess. A smaller synthetic-bristle brush is more suitable for small projects.

Wallpaper brush. Thin and wide, with very short bristles, this is used like a squeegee to work bubbles to the edges of sheets of wallpaper after you apply the sheets to the wall.

Seam roller. This tool is for going over the edges of wallpaper sheets 15 minutes after you install them. On small projects, you can improvise with a finger.

Taping knife. This jumbo-size putty knife is designed for smoothing drywall joint compound; it's helpful when you want to crease wallpaper at room corners so that you can trim the paper neatly. Alternatives are a metal ruler or a straightedge.

Wallpaper sponge. This sponge has small pores that pick up a lot of adhesive residue, and it's easy to clean. Use it to clean stray adhesive from the surface of the wallpaper after you apply it.

Quick Tip: Alternates to PVC

PVC contains plasticizers (flexibility agents) that become airborne over time and create a strong plastic odor that people often find objectionable. Some researchers also link PVC to health and environmental problems. If you have concerns about PVC, ask the store for other options.

How to Hang Mirrors, Shelves, and Accessories

Many projects in this book call for attaching mirrors, shelves, and other items to walls. Here's what you need to know to make sure that what you're fastening to the wall stays fastened.

Drywall

In most homes built since the 1950s, bathroom walls are covered with drywall, a pressed panel with a paper skin and a core of a chalky material known as gypsum.

How to fasten to it. To hang a lightweight item, such as a small picture, use a picture hook and a nail. If you want to hang a shelf, mirror, or other heavy object, however, you need to fasten the object directly to wood or metal framing within the wall (see page 40) or use special anchors (see page 41). This is because gypsum is too crumbly to hold a lot of weight.

Plaster

Bathrooms in older houses are more likely to have walls of plaster, which is harder and more brittle.

How to fasten to it. Plaster is stronger than drywall, so you can fasten medium-weight items directly to the wall. You still need to fasten objects over 20 pounds (including the contents of shelves) or items that will be tugged at—such as hooks for towels—to wood or metal framing, or use anchors (see page 41). Unless you're hammering in a thin nail for a lightweight picture hanger, use screws rather than nails, since hammering can crack plaster and cause it to come loose from the wall. Always drill a hole first, using a bit that's a little narrower than the screw.

Tile

Regardless of what's underneath, bathroom walls are often covered with ceramic, stone, or glass tile.

How to fasten to it. Use a power drill and a bit capable of cutting through the tile. Diamond-core bits cut especially well through the toughest tiles, but some carbide bits also work well, and they cost less. To keep the bit from sliding, place masking tape over the spot where you want to drill. Mist the area with water as you drill, or pause frequently to let the bit cool. Switch to a standard bit once you hit wood (or metal, if your house happens to have metal framing) to finish drilling the hole you need for a screw. If the wall is hollow, use an anchor (see page 41).

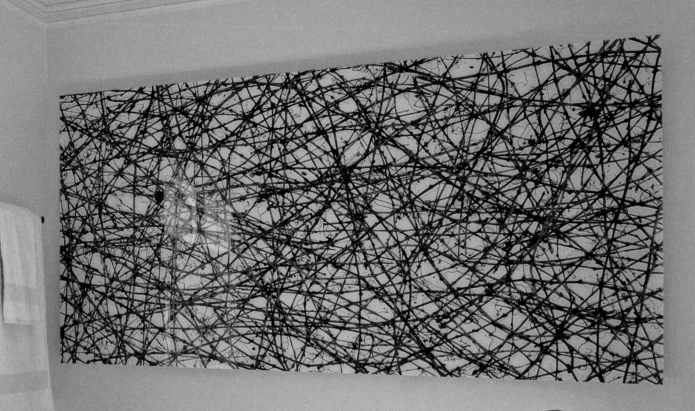

Quick Tip: Drywall Check
If you don't know whether you're working with drywall or plaster, try poking in a pushpin. If it goes in fairly easily, the wall is drywall.

Find the Studs

Behind all drywall and plaster walls lies wood or metal wall framing. Wall framing consists mostly of vertical pieces, called studs, which are just 1½ inch across on the side that faces the room. On drywall or plaster walls, attach heavier items to studs, if it's possible, because the object will be more secure than if you use anchors (see opposite page). But you need to do a little sleuthing to locate the studs.

Look for nail or screw heads. Since baseboards and drywall are nailed or screwed to studs, if you find where they're fastened, you automatically know where the studs are. On baseboard trim, look for nails or patches over nails. On walls, look for divots that line up vertically, showing where someone patched over the fasteners. (If someone did a good job patching over the fasteners, you may not see the divots.)

Tap the wall. If you can't find visible clues, tap sideways across the wall, paying close attention to the sound. When you hear a hollow sound change to a thud, it's a sign that a stud is under-neath. (This is the method recommended in this book because it works on all drywall or plaster walls and doesn't require special equipment.)

Use a sensor. Hardware stores and home centers sell two kinds of sensors: magnetic and electronic. For occasional use, get the magnetic type so you don't have to worry about the batteries wearing down.

Quick Tip: Stud Spacing
Studs are usually spaced with their centerlines 16 inches or 24 inches apart. So once you locate one or two studs on a wall, just measure across to locate the likely position of the other studs.

» **If possible, fasten wood rails like this one to studs in the wall.**

Fasten Items to Studs

If you're fastening directly to framing, here's what to consider.

Screws or nails. You can generally use either nails or screws. Nails go in quicker, but screws are easier to remove, and you don't risk denting the wall with an errant hammer blow. There are a couple of situations, however, where you'd want to use screws: on plaster walls (where nails might cause cracks) and with metal studs.

Length of fastener. Use a fastener length that puts about one-third of the shaft in the piece you're fastening and two-thirds in the piece you're fastening to. On walls, count the drywall or plaster as part of what you're fastening. Therefore, since drywall and plaster are usually ½ or ⅝ inch thick, you need fasteners at least 1½ inches long plus the thickness of whatever you are fastening. However, if you're fastening something that's especially heavy, such as the large mirror mosaic on page 122, you should use even longer screws for extra security.

What You Need to Know About Anchors

When there isn't a stud, and you need to hang something heavy, you need an anchor that's suitable for use in a hollow wall. The best anchor for the job also depends on the weight of what you are hanging. Divide the total weight of what you are hanging (including any contents that will be placed on or in the object) by the number of fasteners. Buy anchors that have at least that load rating, which is often printed on the package. Here are the anchors we recommend.

Plastic expansion anchor

This is a little plastic tube. To install it, just drill a hole matched to the outside diameter of the anchor, press in the anchor, then twist in a screw. The screw pushes against the plastic, causing it to expand and hold tight to the surrounding surface. The connection is only as strong as the material it's pressing against, so this type of anchor works well in stiff materials but isn't strong in ones that are soft.

Use for: light to medium loads on tile and other masonry; light loads on drywall or plaster.

Don't use for: medium to heavy loads on drywall or plaster; light loads on these surfaces when the item will be tugged on, such as towel hooks (page 114) or a toilet-paper holder (page 124).

Molly bolt

Also known as a spreading anchor, this consists of a metal (or sometimes plastic) sleeve and a metal screw. To install, drill a hole sized to the outside diameter of the sleeve. Insert the sleeve and twist in the screw. This causes the sleeve to flare out in the back, permanently anchoring the sleeve to the wall.

Use for: medium to heavy loads on drywall or plaster; tile where there is no stud behind the wall, especially when you may want to take down the item and reinstall it later using the same hardware.

Don't use for: thick masonry; tile where you might want to remove the sleeve later, since the only way to remove a Molly bolt sleeve is by poking it through the wall and into the hollow cavity behind the wall, after first reaming out a hole that's at least as large as the head.

Toggle bolt

The strongest type of anchor but the most difficult to install, this consists of a bolt threaded onto collapsible wings. To install, drill a hole wide enough so you can slip in the bolt with the wings pressed tightly against it. When the wings clear the back of the wall, they spring open. Then you pull out on the bolt until you feel the wings up against the back of the drywall, and tighten the bolt. (Maintaining tension is the tricky part; without that, the wings just twirl around and the bolt never tightens.)

Use for: items mounted to ceilings; medium to heavy loads on walls of drywall, plaster, or tile.

Don't use for: thick masonry or wherever you may want to take down and reinstall the item later using the same hardware, since the wings will fall into the wall cavity once you remove the bolt. (You can, however, install a new toggle bolt in the same hole.)

Build Projects with Wood

If you want to create storage that's tailored to your bathroom, there's no better way than to build the shelves, hook rack, or storage boxes yourself. With simple tools and a little know-how, you can create pieces that are the exact sizes you need (and then paint them the exact colors you want!).

Solid Wood

Solid wood has a natural look, and it's easy to shape with hand tools. There are two broad categories.

Softwood. This comes from conifer trees, including pine, fir, redwood, and cedar. Pine is relatively inexpensive and easy to cut and sand, so it's recommended for many of the projects in this book.

Hardwood. This wood comes mostly from deciduous trees such as oak and maple, and occasionally from broadleaf evergreens, such as madrone. Most, but not all, hardwoods are much stronger and more dent-resistant than softwoods. That's an advantage for things like flooring, but not for projects in this book. You can use oak, maple, or other tough hardwoods for these projects, but be sure to drill holes for all fasteners (pounding in nails might split the wood), and be prepared to spend more time cutting and sanding. Poplar is an exception; though classified as a hardwood, it's as soft as many softwoods and is easy to cut, sand, and nail together. It's fine for any of the projects in this book.

Quick Tip: Make a Wood Rail

If you have a lot of things to hang, cut down on the number of holes you need to drill in your wall (or anchors you need to use) by mounting the components to a wood rail and then attaching that to the wall. See the wooden hook rail project on page 116 to learn how.

Quick Tip: Dark Circles
If you see a dark circle on the end of a board, that was once the center of the tree. The wood is likely to split there, so avoid buying that board.

Shop for Good Wood

There's more to buying a good board than looking for a grain pattern you like. The board also needs to be a workable size, as well as straight and not prone to splitting or cupping. When you buy lumber, you enter a world with its own set of shorthand terms. Everything makes sense—but only if you know the lingo.

Knotty and clear (or knot-free) wood. Knots, which usually look like dark circles on the face of a board, are parts of branches, so the wood grain in them runs perpendicular to the main grain in the board. If the knots are strongly linked to the surrounding wood, they're called "tight knots." Wood with tight knots costs a lot less than clear wood and is fine for all the projects in this book. Avoid boards with loose knots, which are likely to fall out.

Exact dimensions and listed dimensions. The listed thickness and width measurements used to describe boards in a store don't refer to their actual size. Rather, they refer to the size when the wood was freshly cut. But the wood is then dried and smoothed, and it shrinks. So when you purchase wood that is labeled 1 x 2, it will actually be ¾ inch thick and 1½ inches wide. The materials lists in this book refer to listed thickness and width dimensions, so you know what to ask for when you shop. The listed length is the same as the actual length. See the chart below for a quick reference guide.

Lumber sizes

What it's called	What you get
1 x 2	¾" x 1½"
1 x 3	¾" x 2½"
1 x 4	¾" x 3½"
1 x 6	¾" x 5½"
1 x 8	¾" x 7¼"
1 x 10	¾" x 9¼"
1 x 12	¾" x 11¼"
2 x 2	1½" x 1½"

(All of the above numbers refer to thickness x width.)

Orienting Growth Rings

If you're using flat-sawn boards to create boxes or shelving, align the pieces so that the growth rings face out (see below) toward the outside of whatever you are building. The growth rings tend to straighten out as the wood expands, which it will when it gets damp from shower steam, and this orientation will help keep the joints tight.

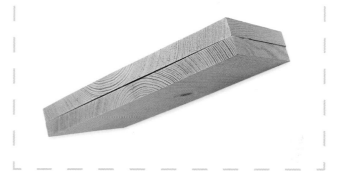

Plywood and MDF

Plywood. This is a piece of wood composed of several thin wood layers that were peeled from a log and glued together. The grain of each layer runs perpendicular to the layers above and below. This makes plywood strong and stable in all directions. Standard sheets are 4 feet by 8 feet, but you can also get it in smaller sizes at home centers.

Medium-density fiberboard. Usually called MDF, this is a type of particleboard made from wood shavings or sawdust. MDF tends to stay flat, but, like all kinds of particleboard, it should not get wet. If it swells, it will never go back to its original size. MDF is also sold primarily in sheets that are 4 feet by 8 feet, but home centers usually sell smaller sizes, too.

Hardboard. Another kind of particleboard, this is typically sold in sheets just ⅛ inch or ¼ inch thick. It's very inexpensive and makes a good base for projects that don't weigh much and that you will completely cover, such as the photo wall on page 146.

Know Your Tools

For the projects in this book, you need only a few basic tools.

Jigsaw. A jigsaw is the best power saw for beginners because it's relatively safe and offers maximum versatility. It cuts curves when it's outfitted with a narrow blade and straight lines if you switch to a wide blade and guide the saw against a straightedge.

Handsaw. This will also work for most of the wood projects in this book (though not for cutting the stars in the star-etched cabinet on page 86). For projects in this book, get a handsaw designed for cutting across the width of a board, not a ripsaw, which is designed for cutting along the length of a board. A saw with 8 to 11 teeth per inch ("tpi" on the label) will work well and leave a smoother edge than a saw with fewer teeth per inch. A short handsaw, about 15 inches long, is easier for beginners to control than one that's the standard length (about 25 inches).

Miter box. This is sometimes used with a handsaw, and helps ensure accurate cuts because it keeps the saw at the correct angle and helps hold the wood steady. You can cut only relatively narrow pieces of wood in a miter box. It works best with a specific kind of handsaw, called a backsaw.

Backsaw. This is a fine-tooth handsaw with a reinforced spine on the top that's designed to cut straight down. It is used with a miter box and is useful for projects like the mirror mosaic (page 122), for which you need to cut pieces of molding.

Quick Tip: Drill a Pilot Hole
Before driving in a screw, drill a hole slightly smaller than the screw shaft. Then drive in the screw. This reduces the risk of splitting the wood, especially when you are working close to the end of a board.

Electric drill. You'll need this to drill holes. If you fit it with a screwdriver tip, you can also use it to drive screws. Corded or cordless work equally well, but a cordless drill is more convenient, provided you keep a spare charged battery at hand. Basic drills often have just two speeds: low, which works best when you're driving in screws, and high, for drilling holes. Always position the bit perpendicular to the wood. When driving in a screw, maintain steady pressure on the drill to prevent the tip from bouncing off.

Combination square. This simple tool helps you mark boards so the ends are perpendicular to the sides, an essential detail if you want to create boxes or boxed shelves with tight, square corners. Measurements are usually stamped into the blade, which makes it easy to mark the shapes you need. But pay attention to where the zero mark is, since it differs depending on which side of the blade you're using.

Hammer. A basic hammer that's not too heavy (16 ounces is a good general-purpose weight) works best for the projects in this book. To avoid bending nails, hammer straight down on the nail head. To work efficiently, professional carpenters always grasp a hammer near the end of the handle. But if you're driving only a few nails, feel free to hold the hammer closer to the head; you'll lose some power but gain more control. To eliminate the risk of denting the wood, hammer against a nailset for the final couple of blows.

Sandpaper or sanding sponges. These simple tools allow you to smooth wood surfaces. See page 30 to see what types are best for which situations.

Pencil. A pencil is necessary for marking cutting lines. Keep the tip sharp, since a dull tip makes such a thick line that it's hard to know exactly where to cut. When you do cut, always leave the line showing, and cut on the side of the line that's on the waste side of the piece. If you cut off the line, you lose your reference mark. Plus, having just a tad extra wood is always good insurance. You can sand off a board that's slightly too long, but you can't stretch one that's a tiny bit too short.

Quick Tip: Practice Makes Perfect
Some sewing steps are difficult to describe but simple
to do, once you understand the general concept. So if
instructions seem confusing, try out the procedures on
scrap fabric or even scrap paper (with tape or staples
instead of stitching).

Get to Know Fabric

Fabric is another way to give new life to your bathroom. Whether you are creating a sink skirt (page 95) or faux Roman shades (page 120), you'll want to take a few things into consideration.

Fabric type. Home decor fabrics tend to be a little wider and heftier than clothing fabrics, and they often have special coatings designed to resist soiling. Washing can remove this coating, so if you are sewing something that you plan to launder, shop for fabric in the store area devoted to clothing and quilting. If you are sewing something that will need only occasional shaking out (or vacuuming or tumbling in a dryer set on no heat), explore the decor fabrics, too.

Patterns. Solid-color or textured fabrics are easiest for beginning sewers because mistakes won't be as evident. With a pattern such as stripes, though, it will be more noticeable if the stripes don't line up across the seams. Plaids are the most complicated of all because they have vertical and horizontal lines that need to line up precisely in a finished piece.

Weight. Heavyweight fabrics tend to be the most durable, but they're not always the best choice because home sewing machines may not be able to pierce through numerous layers of fabric.

Stretchability. For most home decor projects, the best fabric is one that does not easily stretch. Avoid knits, and focus on woven fabrics. Before you buy, test a few fabrics you like by tugging a corner lengthwise, crosswise, and at a 45-degree angle. The less the shape changes, the easier the fabric will be to sew.

Know Your Tools

Only a few tools are needed for sewing, but it's important to have the correct ones. Here's the short list.

Needles. Whether you are sewing by hand or machine, choose a thin needle for sewing lightweight fabric and a thick needle for sewing bulkier fabric. For hand sewing, you can use a "sharp," a general-purpose needle of medium length and with a small, rounded eye. If you prefer a shorter needle or will be making a lot of tiny stitches, use a style of needle called a "between." Embroidery needles, which are longer than sharps and have an oval eye, are helpful for making a lot of long stitches (see the sink skirt on

page 95) or when using thick thread. For machine sewing, match the tip shape to the type of fabric and the eye size to the type of thread. If you are using home-decor woven fabric, use a sharp tip and size 14/80 needle, and change the needle frequently so it won't become dull.

Thread. If you want stitches to blend in to the fabric color, choose a thread color that is slightly darker than the main color of the fabric. If you're combining several fabrics, say a print and a stripe, choose a thread color that is common to both. Either cotton or polyester thread is fine for the projects in this book.

Scissors. The fabric projects in this book involve cutting long, straight pieces of fabric, so use scissors with long blades, about 8 to 9 inches. Bent-handle shears are ideal because they allow the fabric to remain flat while you cut it. For clipping threads, use a small pair of scissors, maybe 4 to 5 inches long. Whatever the size or style, scissors blades need to be sharp. If yours aren't, have them resharpened.

Sewing machine. Although it's possible to sew anything with just a needle and thread, you'll get more uniform stitches and save time with a sewing machine.

Notions. Fabric stores are well stocked with items that make sewing easier and more fun, such as iron-on seam tape, corded trim, and markers with ink that fades on its own. If you're doing a lot of sewing, check out all the goodies that are available.

Enjoy the Journey

It can be easy to become overly focused on doing things right —or getting them done quickly. Try to remember that mistakes are par for the course and sometimes yield surprisingly interesting results. Above all, have fun!

> **Quick Tip: Stay On Grain**
> If you are using fabric with a print, make sure the design is on grain, meaning that it runs parallel to the selvages (the woven-in edges). If the design is not on grain, your project will look crooked.

3

Transform your bath with paint and wallpaper

Bathrooms are smaller than most rooms in the house, which makes them easy—and affordable—to make over. With a couple of cans of color or a small amount of wallpaper, you can take your bathroom from dingy to dazzling in the space of a weekend—and sometimes less. This chapter will show you how to do everything from repainting your bathroom to updating vanity cabinets and creating a playful striped floor. Just follow our step-by-step instructions, and change the whole look and feel of your bathroom.

Soft and Lush ⌄

If you have wood paneling in your bathroom, use different colors for the different sections of paneling. In this pretty palette, the bottom half of the room is powder blue and the top half is cream. For contrast, add another color, like the green lamp.

Vibrant Color ⌃

Transform your space with a burst of color. Try a turquoise, like this one, or even a deep purple or rich magenta. Paint the trim a simple white for contrast. See instructions for painting an entire bathroom (page 56), painting trim (page 60), and painting windows (page 62).

« Stripe It

If you like stripes, paint them on the wall. For bathrooms with a low ceiling, this clean, chic, and fun look will also make the ceiling look higher. To learn how to paint stripes on a floor, see page 72.

Sunny Wallpaper ⌄

With a fresh wallpaper pattern like this one, you can make an ordinary space feel warm and inviting. Yellow is especially nice in a space that gets a hint of natural light. Learn how to wallpaper an accent wall in your own bathroom on page 66.

Chic Accent Wall »

If you love bright hues but don't want to overwhelm the space with color, paint just one wall—or even just part of one. Pair a rich color like this green with a bright white for contrast. For full instructions on painting an accent wall, see page 64.

Luminous Look »

If you're lucky enough to have a bathroom that's flooded with sunshine, choose colors that reflect the light but won't cause glare. These lavender walls are an attractive backdrop to the silver-painted tub. See page 68 to learn more about tub painting.

($) ($)

Repainted bathroom

Repainting your bathroom with fresh colors can be like taking a magic wand to the room, instantly brightening and infusing the space with new life.

First-Timer Tips

» Because kitchen and bath paint is somewhat glossy, overlapping wet paint on dry paint can leave visible lines when the wet paint dries. The solution: Work in small, consecutive sections to avoid overlap.

» On a ceiling that's not square, paint across the room's shorter dimension so that the paint in each section will still be wet when you start the next. This will make the transitions look seamless.

Materials

- patch material (see page 28 for type)
- wall texture spray (for textured walls that need patching)
- primer (if needed; see page 32)
- satin (or a glossier finish) kitchen and bath paint for ceiling and walls, 1 quart per 500 square feet (for two coats)
- gloss or semi-gloss latex enamel for trim, 1 quart per 100 square feet

Tools

- drop cloths
- ladder or step stool
- microfiber dust cloth
- two or three safety pins
- broom or dust mop
- rubber gloves, bucket, and sponge
- household cleaner, or deglosser if existing paint has a gloss finish
- putty knife
- sandpaper or sanding sponge, 180 grit and coarser, as needed
- vacuum
- synthetic-bristle brush, 1½ inch or 2 inch
- paint tray
- roller, 9 inch, preferably with an extendable handle (for ceiling)
- painter's masking tape, 1 inch or wider

continued on page 58

▶ Steps

1. Prep

Take down the shower curtain and window coverings, and cover the floor, countertops, and bathtub with the drop cloths. Shut off the power at the circuit breaker, check that the power is off with a circuit tester, and then remove the switch covers and light fixture(s) if necessary. Clean cobwebs and lint from the ceiling, walls, and top edges of the trim with the microfiber dust cloth pinned around the broom or dust mop. Wearing gloves, wash all the surfaces you plan to paint with water and the cleaner or deglosser. Remove residue, and let dry.

2. Patch

With the putty knife, use the patch material to fill any gouges. Let dry. Sand the patches flat; start with 100 grit, then go to 150 grit. On woodwork, make a final pass with 180 grit. Vacuum up the sanding residue. If the walls are textured, apply wall texture spray to any patches.

3. Prime

If you are priming only the patches, use the synthetic-bristle brush to apply the primer. If you are priming the entire surface, prime in the same manner that you'll be painting each section of the room, following the instructions below. Let the primer dry.

4. Paint the ceiling

With the synthetic-bristle brush, apply a band of ceiling paint about 2 inches wide to the ceiling edges in an area about 4 feet wide. Make sure the paint reaches all the way into the corners, even if some gets onto the walls. Then use the roller to fill in the main expanse of the ceiling in that area. Make the final passes in straight lines. Work your way across the ceiling in similar-size sections. Let dry. Apply a second coat if the label says it's necessary. Reinstall the ceiling fixtures.

5. Mask the walls

Unless the wall paint matches the ceiling paint, apply painter's masking tape on the ceiling close to where it meets the walls. Also tape off any trim or other surfaces, such as tile, that you won't be painting. Press the tape firmly down on the edge that faces the walls you will be painting.

6. Paint the walls

Again, work in sections about 4 feet wide. First, use the brush to paint a band about 2 inches wide along the top and the base of the wall. Then roll a thick N shape onto the top half of that wall section. Even out the paint by rolling up and down through the N in straight lines. Paint the lower area in the same way. Finish by running the roller (without reloading it with paint) from the top of the wall to the bottom in a single pass. At the corners, switch to the brush. Complete the rest of the sections on that wall. Paint the remaining walls in the same way. When you are painting the second wall of each corner, pull the brush back horizontally so you don't leave drips or smear the wall you just painted. Let dry. If the label recommends two coats, or if the paint looks thin or blotchy when dry, add a second coat. Once the paint dries, remove the tape. Reinstall the switch covers and restore the power.

7. Paint the trim and cabinets

With the brush and the latex enamel, paint the windows first (page 62). Then paint the window trim (page 62). If you're in a hurry to use the room, you can move back most of the furnishings and take your time painting the doors and the vanity or other cabinets (pages 74 and opposite).

($)

Repainted vanity cabinets

Do you dream of new vanity cabinets but don't want to contend with swapping out the plumbing or investing in a new countertop? There's an easier way to get a fresh new look: Just paint the cabinets you have.

Materials

- wood filler (if wood needs patching)
- primer for slick surfaces
- gloss or semi-gloss latex paint or latex enamel, 1 quart per 50 square feet (to allow two coats)

Tools

- drop cloths
- painter's masking tape, 1 inch or wider
- screwdriver
- pencil
- rubber gloves, bucket, and sponge
- household cleaner, or deglosser if existing paint has a gloss finish
- putty knife (to apply wood filler)
- sandpaper or sanding sponge, 100 grit and 180 grit
- microfiber dust cloth
- synthetic-bristle brush, 1½ inch or 2 inch

Steps

1. Prep

Apply tape to any adjacent surfaces that won't be painted. Remove the cabinet drawers and, with the screwdriver, remove the knobs. With the pencil, number the drawers (on the bottoms) and number their corresponding locations in the cabinet. Place the drawers face up on a drop cloth. Wearing gloves, wash the drawers with water and the cleaner or deglosser. Let dry.

2. Smooth the surfaces

With the putty knife, press wood filler into any nicks. When the filler dries, sand the patches smooth with 100-grit sandpaper or the sanding sponge. With the 180-grit sandpaper or sanding sponge, scuff all the surfaces. Remove residue with the dust cloth.

3. Prime

Working on one drawer at a time, brush on the primer. Start from the center of the drawer. First paint the center panel, then the bevel around it. Then work out to the edges of the drawer front. As you complete each part, brush away any drips. Repeat for all the drawers. Position a drop cloth beneath the cabinet. Brush primer onto the remaining cabinet areas, in the direction of the wood grain. Let dry.

4. Paint and complete

Apply the paint in the same way. After the first coat dries, apply a second coat. Let dry. Remove the tape, reattach the knobs, and replace the drawers.

($)

Painted trim

Think of trim as a bathroom's jewelry—the finishing touch that sets the style, adds a little flair, and pulls different elements together. Paint your trim a color that contrasts with the rest of the bathroom and change the whole look of the space.

Materials

- wood filler (if trim needs patching)
- primer (if needed; see page 32)
- gloss or semi-gloss latex enamel

Tools

- drop cloths
- ladder or step stool
- painter's masking tape, 1 inch or wider
- putty knife (to apply wood filler)
- household cleaner, or deglosser if existing paint has a gloss finish
- rubber gloves, bucket, and sponge
- sandpaper or sanding sponge, 180 grit (plus 100 grit if you need to patch)
- microfiber dust cloth
- synthetic-bristle brush, 1 inch or 2 inch, preferably angled

Steps

1. Prep

Take down any window treatment or shower curtain next to any trim you will be painting, and position the drop cloths. Apply the painter's masking tape to protect the surrounding surfaces, and press down firmly along all edges facing the trim. Patch any holes or dents in the trim, using the putty knife and wood filler. Let the wood filler dry, then sand it smooth with the coarser sandpaper or sanding sponge.

2. Wash and scuff

Wearing gloves, wash the trim with water and the cleaner or deglosser. When the surface is dry, lightly scuff up the paint with the finer sandpaper or sanding sponge, and wipe away the residue with the dust cloth.

3. Prime

If there is oil paint on the trim (see page 33 for how to test it) or if you are switching between light and dark colors, you need to prime. (Otherwise, go to step 4.) Apply the primer with the brush, taking care to get into any curved surfaces. Moving from the top trim to the bottom trim, complete each section before you go on to the next. End with the door trim. Let dry.

4. Paint

Apply the latex enamel with the brush, using the same method described in step 3. To ensure a smooth coat on trim pieces that are too long to paint in one stroke (especially if you are working on a ladder), begin painting at one end or corner and gradually lift up on the brush as you complete the stroke. Begin the next stroke a workable distance beyond the end of the first stroke, and brush toward the first section you painted. After the overlap, gradually lift up on the brush. Continue painting in this manner until you have painted the entire piece of trim. Then go on to the next piece. End with the door trim. Let dry.

5. Recoat

Inspect the paint. If you see gaps, apply a second coat. Do not apply a second coat unless it is needed, though, since too many layers of paint will obscure the trim's details.

First-Timer Tips

» Paint the trim at the top of the wall first and work your way down. This avoids the risk of dripping paint onto a surface that you just painted.

» If your bathroom has a pocket door (as pictured here), you'll need to take the door out of the frame to paint it. To remove the door, release the locking tab at the top and then lift the door to disengage the hardware it hangs on.

($)

Painted windows

Lots of homes have double-hung windows in the bathroom. Here's how to make yours sing with a new paint job.

Materials
- wood filler (if wood needs patching)
- primer (if needed; see step 4)
- gloss or semi-gloss latex enamel

Tools
- screwdriver
- drop cloth
- ladder or step stool
- paint scraper, if needed
- putty knife (to apply wood filler)
- damp cloth
- rubber gloves, bucket, and sponge
- bleach (if existing paint is stained)
- cleaning cloth (if you use bleach)
- household cleaner, or deglosser if existing paint has a gloss finish
- sandpaper or sanding sponge, 180 grit
- microfiber dust cloth
- painter's masking tape, 1 inch or wider
- angled synthetic-bristle brush, 1 inch to 1½ inch
- double-edge razor blade

▶ Steps

1. Prep

Remove any window coverings and nearby furnishings. With the screwdriver, remove all the window hardware. Position the drop cloth. With the paint scraper, remove any loose paint, particularly below each glass section where moisture collects. If a window doesn't open and close smoothly, repair it before you paint. (Often, all it takes is sliding a wide putty knife between the sash and the molding to break a paint seal.)

2. Clean and scuff

With the damp cloth, wipe off any mildew from the window frames and trim. Wearing gloves and using the cleaning cloth, clean off any stains on the paint with a solution of 3 parts water to 1 part bleach. Rinse well. Then wash the paint with water and the cleaner or deglosser; when the surface is dry, lightly scuff up the paint with the sandpaper or sanding sponge, and wipe away the residue with the dust cloth. (Caution: Do not mix the bleach with any cleaner that contains ammonia, and avoid getting deglosser on glass.)

3. Patch and mask

Fill any small holes in the wood with wood filler. Smooth the patches with the putty knife. When the filler is dry, sand lightly if needed. Apply the painter's masking tape to the glass and to the wall surrounding the window. Press the tape down firmly along edges where you will paint. At the corners of the glass, press the putty knife over the tape, then neatly tear the tape off along the knife edge.

4. Prime

Brush primer over any bare spots, or spackle the patches. If the old paint is oil based (see page 33 for how to test it) or if you are switching from a dark to a light color, prime the entire surface, following the same procedure used for painting in step 5. Let dry.

5. Paint the sash

Use the brush to paint the sashes (the moveable window sections) with the latex enamel. First lower the upper sash. Then raise the lower sash enough so you can reach the bottom edge of the upper sash and paint the surface that faces the room but is covered when the window is closed. Then close both window sections most of the way and paint the remaining surfaces that face the room, as well as the top edge of the bottom sash. Paint from the inside out, painting any dividers between the glass before you paint the frame. Avoid painting the top edge of the top sash and the bottom edge of the bottom sash. Leave both sashes slightly ajar until the paint dries completely.

6. Paint the remaining parts

Paint the molding around the sash, but do not get paint in the recess where the window moves up and down. Finally, paint the window trim, starting at the top and working down. Remove the tape. Use the razor blade to remove any paint that has seeped onto the glass.

Maintenance Tip

To keep your newly painted window from sticking, rub a little mineral oil on the molding edge facing the sash, and try to open and close the window daily for the first month. (It takes that long for latex paint to harden.)

Alternate Method

If you are painting windows framed with vinyl or aluminum, the procedure is different. Wash vinyl with a TSP substitute; wash aluminum with a little distilled white vinegar. Then use a water-based primer suitable for slick surfaces and a latex enamel as the finish paint.

($)

Accent wall

If you've been itching to paint your bathroom a wild, bright color but don't want to overwhelm the room, paint an accent wall. The best wall to accent: The one where your eye naturally goes.

Materials
- primer (if needed; see page 32)
- satin or semi-gloss latex paint, 1 quart per 100 square feet

Tools
- drop cloths
- ladder or step stool
- rubber gloves, bucket, and sponge
- household cleaner, or deglosser if existing paint has a gloss finish
- painter's masking tape, 1 inch or wider
- synthetic-bristle brush, 1½ inch or 2 inch
- paint tray
- roller, 9 inch
- artist's brush

First-Timer Tip
When you apply painter's masking tape to protect the ceiling and adjacent walls, place the tape just beyond the wall you will paint rather than attempt to align it in the exact corners, which will likely be a bit rounded.

Steps

1. Prep
Position the drop cloths. Wearing gloves, wash the wall with water and the cleaner or deglosser.

2. Tape
To avoid smearing paint on the surrounding surfaces, apply the painter's masking tape to the ceiling, baseboard, and walls on both sides of the accent wall. Place the tape just beyond the accent wall. Press down firmly on the tape edges that face the accent wall.

3. Patch and prime
If you need to patch holes, see the instructions on page 58. Then, prime the patches using the synthetic-bristle brush. To prime the rest of the surface, use the brush to apply a band of primer about 2 inches wide along the taped edges. To keep the primer from bleeding under the tape, direct the brush away from the tape. Next, pour primer into the paint tray. With the roller, prime the main expanse of the accent wall, working on sections about 3 feet across at a time. First prime the top of each section by rolling on primer in an N shape. Then roll vertically to even out the primer. In the same way, prime the lower part of the section. Finally, run the nearly dry roller from the top of the wall to the bottom. Go over the primer only once this way, then let it dry.

4. Paint
Apply the latex paint to the wall, using the same procedure you used in step 3. After you roll from the top of the wall to the bottom in each area, avoid going back to touch up areas that look thin. Let dry.

5. Touch up and complete
If the paint looks thin or blotchy when dry, add a second coat. Let the paint dry again. Then remove the tape carefully. With the artist's brush, touch up any places where paint seeped under the tape or the tape pulled away the paint.

Style Note
If your accent wall is an unusual color, it may be hard to find accessories to match. The solution: Paint a few simple pieces, such as a tissue box or planter box, with some of the leftover paint.

(\$)(\$)

Wallpaper accent wall

Wallpaper an accent wall and brighten up your whole bathroom.

Materials

- drywall mud or spackle (if wall needs patching)
- acrylic wallcovering primer with sizing
- pre-pasted wallpaper

Tools

- plastic drop cloths
- ladder or step stool
- rubber gloves, bucket, and sponge
- household cleaner
- putty knife (to apply patch material)
- paint and water trays
- roller, 9 inch or mini
- synthetic-bristle brush, 1½ inch or 2 inch
- scissors
- tape measure and pencil
- carpenter's level
- wallpaper brush
- seam roller
- wallpaper sponge
- taping knife, 6 inch to 10 inch
- single-edge razor blade

▶ Steps

1. Prep and prime

Position the drop cloths. Wearing gloves, wash the wall with water and the cleaner. Let dry. To patch any holes, apply the drywall mud or spackle with the putty knife. Let dry. Pour some primer with sizing into the tray and prime the wall, using the roller. At corners, switch to the synthetic-bristle brush. Let dry.

2. Find the starting point

With the tape measure and the pencil, measure the wall's width and mark the midpoint. Then, using the wallpaper roll as a guide, mark wallpaper-width increments across the wall from the midpoint to the edges. If less than half the paper's width is left over at each corner, plan to center the first strip over the wall's midpoint (see top illustration). Otherwise, plan to have the first two pieces flank the wall's midpoint (see bottom illustration). In either case, use the pencil and the carpenter's level to draw a vertical line ¼ inch to the left of where the left edge of the first strip will be (so the pencil mark won't show in the seam).

Find the starting point

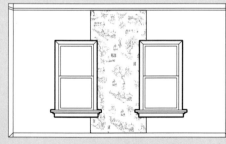

Center the first strip over the wall's midpoint.

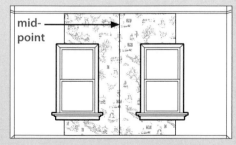

Place the first two pieces so they flank the wall's midpoint.

3. Cut the paper

Measure the wall's height. On the floor, unroll a length of the paper. Choose what part of the pattern you want at the top of the wall. Allowing an extra 2 inches at the top and bottom, cut off the strip with the scissors. Unroll another length of wallpaper, line up the pattern with the first strip, and cut to length. Repeat for the remaining pieces.

4. Paste

Roll one of the strips so the pasted side faces out. Add water to the wallpaper water tray. Submerge the rolled strip in the water. Grab the paper's top edge and lift the sheet from the water as it unrolls. Place the strip right side down on the drop cloths. Loosely fold the top and bottom edges toward the center (a process known as "booking"), so no sticky side faces out. Wait the recommended booking time.

5. Apply

Unfold the top half of the paper and align it with 2 inches extra at the top, ¼ inch to the right of the guide line (from step 2). Working your way down, smooth the paper against the wall with your fingertips and the wallpaper brush. Brush from the center toward the sides. Prepare and position the remaining sheets in the same way, butting the edges tightly together. About 15 minutes after you apply each sheet, roll over the edges with the seam roller. Wipe the wallpaper with the damp wallpaper sponge.

6. Trim

To trim the top and bottom edges, place the taping knife over the wallpaper and press the tool's thin edge into the corner. Trace against the edge with the razor blade, neatly slicing off the excess.

First-Timer Tip

Make sure the wallpaper you use is suitable for a bathroom's humid environment.

$

Painted tub

A claw-foot tub looks luxurious no matter what, but painting it a bright color gives your bathroom a playful, modern feel.

Materials
- rust-bonding primer (only if there's rust)
- shellac-based primer
- latex enamel, 1 quart

Tools
- drop cloths
- rubber gloves, bucket, and sponge-type scrub pad
- household cleaner, or deglosser if existing paint has a gloss finish
- painter's masking tape, 1 inch or wider
- synthetic-bristle brush, 1½ inch
- paint tray
- mini roller

Style Note
For a chic look, paint the feet a contrasting color. White feet look especially sharp on a tub with a white interior. Metallic paints also work.

Steps

1. Wash
You'll be painting only the exterior of the tub. Check that any existing exterior paint is intact and not flaking off. (If it is flaking, you'll need to have the tub stripped or sandblasted first so the new paint won't peel.) Position the drop cloths. Wearing gloves, wash the exterior of the tub with water and the cleaner. Clean as much of the outside of the tub as you have access to. Let dry.

2. Apply the tape
Apply the painter's masking tape to the top edge of the tub feet or to the floor around the feet, depending on whether you are leaving the feet with their existing finish or are painting them. Also apply tape along the top rim of the tub, to keep the interior paint-free.

3. Treat the rust
Inspect the tub exterior, and the feet if you plan to paint them. If you find rust, use the brush to apply the rust-bonding primer over those areas (this chemically converts the rust so the paint will bond to the surface).

4. Prep and prime the surface
Don't sand, as you normally might before priming, because the existing paint is likely to contain lead. Pour the shellac-based primer into the paint tray, and use the roller to paint the main areas of the tub. Then use the brush to smooth out the finish and fill in where the roller won't reach, such as the underside of the tub rim. Prime the feet, too, if you plan to paint them.

5. Paint the exterior and feet
Apply the latex enamel in the same way you applied the primer in step 4. (Skip the feet if you'll paint them a contrasting color—see Style Note.) When the first coat dries, apply a second coat if needed. Let dry.

First-Timer Tips

» If you need to paint a tub that is close to a wall, wear long rubber gloves when reaching between the wall and tub (to protect your arm from paint) and consider using a sponge to apply the paint.

» Don't worry if you leave gaps along a tub edge that you can't see. The paint is just for show, so gaps you can't see don't matter.

Steps

($)

Multicolored vanity cabinets

Have a plain, laminate-faced vanity in a bathroom? Give it a whole new personality in just a few hours with some fun paint and a little elbow grease.

Materials

- primer for slick surfaces
- different colors of gloss or semi-gloss latex enamel, sample size or quarts

Tools

- pencil
- drop cloth or newspapers
- screwdriver
- rubber gloves, bucket, and sponge
- deglosser
- sandpaper or sanding sponge, 180 grit
- microfiber dust cloth
- painter's masking tape, any width (optional)
- paint tray
- mini roller
- synthetic-bristle brush, 1 inch or 1½ inch

1. Prep

Empty the drawers you want to paint, and remove them from the vanity. Use the pencil to number each one on the back to identify where it fits. Set the drawers, front side up, on the drop cloth or newspapers. Using the screwdriver, detach the handles. Set them and the screws aside. Wearing gloves, wash the drawer fronts and their surrounding edges with water and the deglosser. Let dry.

2. Scuff

Lightly sand the drawer fronts and their edges. Sand just enough to scuff up the surface. (If you want to paint the cabinet case itself, scuff up its exterior as well.) Wipe away the residue with the microfiber dust cloth.

3. Tape (optional)

To keep primer and enamel from smearing onto the back of the drawer fronts, affix painter's masking tape to the back side of the drawer fronts, along the outer edges. Press down on the tape edges that face the surface you will be painting. (If you have a steady hand, you can skip this step. It's not as crucial as in some painting projects since here you have a crisp edge to paint along. Also, smears are easy to wipe off laminate, provided you do it promptly.)

4. Prime

Pour primer into the paint tray. Apply it to the drawer fronts, using the mini roller. Use the brush to wipe away drips and to coat the top, bottom, and side edges of the drawer fronts. Let dry.

5. Paint

Pour one color of latex enamel into the paint tray. With the roller, paint one drawer front. Switch to the brush to paint the edges and wipe away any drips. Clean the tools, then paint the next color on the next drawer front and edges. Repeat for the remaining drawers. Let dry, then reattach the handles. Slide the drawers back into the vanity.

Style Note

For added flair, apply vinyl decals, or stencil a geometric pattern onto some or all of the drawers.

$ $

Striped floor

Walls are not the only place to play with paint. To make your bathroom cheerful, color-stripe the floor. For extra flair, mottle one color of the stripes.

Materials

- primer (if recommended for the floor paint)
- eggshell or satin latex porch and floor paint, two colors (for stripes)
- clear latex glaze
- latex paint in a contrasting color (to tint glaze)

Tools

- rubber gloves, bucket, and sponge-type scrub pad
- household cleaner, or deglosser if the existing paint has a gloss finish
- random-orbit or finish sander with 120-grit or 150-grit sandpaper
- vacuum
- painter's masking tape, 1 inch or wider
- paint tray and mini roller
- synthetic-bristle brush, 2 inch to 3 inch, depending on stripe width
- plastic container, quart size or larger
- measuring cup
- disposable gloves and plastic bowl
- natural sponge and newspaper

▶ Steps

1. Clean
Wearing the rubber gloves, wash the floor with water and the cleaner or deglosser. Wipe away all residue. Let dry.

2. Sand
Scuff-sand the floor with the sander, just enough to make it evenly dull. Vacuum.

3. Prep and prime
Apply the painter's masking tape along the lower edge of the baseboard, and press the bottom edge down well. If the paint label recommends a primer, apply it now. Pour the primer into the paint tray and apply it with the roller, followed by a few smoothing strokes with the synthetic-bristle brush. Start in the corner farthest from the door and paint toward the door. Let dry.

4. Paint the first color
Decide how wide you want the stripes and mark their edges on the painter's masking tape on the baseboard. With the roller, paint the whole floor the color that you won't mottle (this is white in the photo). Or, if the stripes are wide, just paint strips a little wider than you want them to wind up. After you roll on the paint for each area or stripe, use the brush, nearly dry, to even out the finish. Go over each area only once or twice, easing up on the brush at the end of each pass. Let dry.

5. Paint the second color
Using the marks you made in step 4 as a guide, apply the painter's masking tape to define the stripes. Place the tape on the color you applied in step 4, with the outside edge of the tape along the transition line. Press down firmly on each tape edge that faces an unpainted stripe. Then apply the second color of floor paint. Let dry.

6. Prep for mottling
Fill the bucket halfway with water. In the quart-size plastic container, mix the contrasting paint (about 1 cup for most bathroom floors) with twice to four times as much glaze, depending on the color you want, to create the tinted glaze. Put on the disposable gloves and pour some of the tinted glaze into the plastic bowl.

7. Mottle
Dampen and wring out the sponge. Dip the tips of the sponge into the glaze in the plastic bowl. Blot the sponge by dabbing it on newspaper. Then apply the glaze to one of the stripes you painted in step 5. Dab up and down; don't rub. Rinse, wring out, and reload the sponge as needed, always blotting before you continue on the stripe. When you complete one stripe, remove the tape along its edges and wipe off any glaze that smeared onto the adjoining paint-only stripe. Repeat for all the stripes you want to mottle. Let dry.

Style Note
For this project, a subtle effect will look best. Tint the glaze with a color that's just a few shades darker than the base paint.

First-Timer Tips
» If the floor is already painted, lightly hand-sand an inconspicuous area, wipe up the dust, and then brush on a little paint. Let dry. If the new paint wrinkles or lifts, the floor can't be painted unless a professional floor finisher strips it first.

» You can walk on the floor in stocking feet once the paint dries, but don't allow it to get wet for at least a week. Wait a couple of weeks before you cover the floor with a bath mat for long periods, so the paint can cure.

Painted door

Bring warmth and a welcoming feeling to your bathroom by painting the door a beautiful color.

Materials

- primer (if needed; see step 3)
- gloss or semi-gloss latex enamel, 1 quart (main color)
- gloss latex enamel, sample size (contrast color)

Tools

- drop cloth or newspaper
- rubber gloves, bucket, and sponge-type scrub pad
- household cleaner, or deglosser if existing paint has a gloss finish
- sandpaper or sanding sponge, 180 grit
- vacuum
- painter's masking tape, no wider than the bevels on the door panels
- screwdriver
- synthetic-bristle brush, 2 inch or 2½ inch
- paint tray
- mini roller

▶Steps

1. Prep the surface

Check that any existing paint on the door is intact and is not flaking off. (If it is flaking, you'll need to get the door stripped first or the new paint will peel.) Position the drop cloth. If the door is painted, put on gloves and wash the door with water and the cleaner or deglosser. Let dry, and then lightly scuff up the paint with the sandpaper or sanding sponge, but avoid sanding through the paint. Vacuum up the debris or wipe it off with the sponge.

2. Prep the hardware

Cover the door hinges with the painter's masking tape. With the screwdriver, remove the doorknob, or leave it in place and mask it, too. The latter approach is safer on an old door because the knob assembly may be tricky to reinstall.

3. Prime the door

If there is oil-based paint on the door (see page 33 for how to test it), or if you are switching from a dark to a light color, you need to prime. (Otherwise, skip this step.) Apply the primer using the same procedure described for the latex paint in steps 4 and 5 below, but prime the bevels around each panel just before you prime the panel itself.

4. Paint the outer edges and panels

With the brush, apply the main color of enamel to the right, left, and top edges of the door. As you finish each edge, run the nearly dry brush along the corners to smooth out any drips. Switch to the roller to paint the main part of each panel. As you complete each panel, go over the enamel immediately with a series of long, side-by-side brush strokes. It's okay to get enamel into the bevels, but brush away any drips.

5. Paint the door frame

Brush the paint around the doorknob, if it's still in place. Then paint the frames surrounding the panels, using the same roller and brush combination as in step 4. If there is a flat section at the center, paint it first. Paint the top horizontal piece next, then the verticals down as far as the next horizontal, and then the next horizontal. In this manner, work your way down the door. Repeat steps 4 and 5 on the other side of the door. Let dry.

6. Paint the bevels

Just beyond the bevels, apply the painter's masking tape to the door frame and panels. Press down the tape along the edge that faces the bevels. With the brush, paint each bevel. Brush from one corner to the approximate center of a section, then brush in the opposite direction from the other corner toward the center. After the overlap, gradually lift the brush. This procedure prevents drips in corners and creates a smooth overlap. Let dry.

7. Touch up and complete

If the enamel looks thin or blotchy when dry, touch up any gaps with the brush or add a second coat.

Style Tip

If a door connects two rooms, consider painting each side of the door to match the room it faces when it's closed. (Remember, though, that when a door is open, its "inside" face looks out on the other room, so choose colors with that in mind.)

Alternate Method

Remove the door before you paint. It's trickier to do, but it reduces the risk of drips and allows you to take off the hinges for cleaning or refinishing. Removing a panel door involves heavy lifting, so line up a friend to help.

($)

Wallpaper cabinet doors

Why not make your functional cabinet doors prettier to look at? Wallpaper them with a lively pattern and bring a fresh feel to your bathroom.

Materials

- wallpaper remnant, or 1 double roll of new wallpaper, pre-pasted or unpasted
- acrylic wallcovering primer with sizing
- clear strippable wallcovering adhesive labeled for all wallcovering types (if wallpaper is unpasted)

Tools

- ruler
- drafting triangle
- pencil
- sticky notes (Post-Its)
- scissors
- rubber gloves, bucket, and sponge
- household cleaner, or deglosser if existing paint has a gloss finish
- synthetic-bristle brush, 2 inch
- smoothing tool or wallpaper brush
- wallpaper sponge

Steps

1. Measure and cut

With the ruler, measure the door panels. Then, using the ruler, drafting triangle, and pencil, lightly outline the shapes on the face of the wallpaper. On the sticky notes, mark the placement of the shapes and which end of each shape will face the top of the cabinet door. With the scissors, cut the wallpaper exactly to fit.

2. Clean

Wearing gloves, wash the door with water and the cleaner or deglosser. Let dry.

3. Apply the primer with sizing

With the synthetic-bristle brush, apply a thin, even coat of wall-covering primer with sizing to each door panel. (This helps the wallpaper stick to glossy paint, which is commonly used on cabinet doors. The primer with sizing also makes the wallpaper easier to remove later.) Wipe away any drips with the damp wallpaper sponge. Let dry.

4. Apply the wallpaper

If the wallpaper is unpasted, use the clean brush to apply a thin, even coat of the adhesive onto one door panel. (If you're using pre-pasted paper, brush water, instead of adhesive, onto the back of the paper and wait for the "booking time" recommended by the wallpaper manufacturer. This delay allows the adhesive to absorb enough moisture to become active.) In either case, press the wallpaper onto the door panel. If you see that the paper isn't aligned properly, shift it into position. Smooth the paper with your fingers as you go. Then go over the sheet with the smoothing tool or wallpaper brush, working from the center toward the edges. Sponge off any excess adhesive with the wallpaper sponge. Repeat for the other door panels.

5. Finish up

After applying wallpaper to each panel, wait about 15 minutes and then press around the edges of the wallpaper with your fingers one more time. Wipe the surface again with the wallpaper sponge.

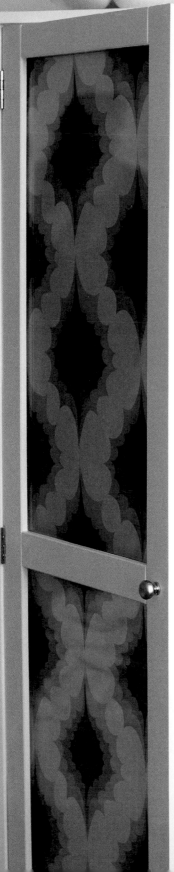

Alternate Method

Instead of pasting the wallpaper to the door panels, you can use permanent double-face tape. The upside is that it's a bit neater to do; the downside is that the tape is harder to remove than the wallpaper paste if you change your mind later on.

Money-Saving Tip

A typical minimum order of new wallpaper is a double roll of 11 yards or more. To get a smaller amount, search online for "wallpaper by the yard" to find companies that sell shorter lengths, or check out yard sales for smaller portions of vintage paper.

4

Creative storage

Most bathrooms need to store a lot of stuff, from cosmetics and towels to rubber duckies and shampoo bottles. But there's not always a wealth of space in a bathroom. That's why it's important to be creative when it comes to storage. In this chapter, you will learn how to use fabric, wood, paint, and a few simple tools to create all kinds of stylish storage options. With projects like a pretty sink skirt, wooden box shelves, and star-etched ventilated cabinets, your bathroom can now be both practical *and* beautiful.

In the Basket ⌄

This book is about building projects, but you can also create storage by adding simple accessories. Use woven baskets like these to hold towels or toiletries. This works especially well in a guest bathroom, where you may want to keep towels where visitors can easily find them.

Clever Storage ⌃

With this smart idea, you can keep your TP easily accessible. See page 124 for a stylish toilet-paper-holder idea that uses pipe fittings and vibrant hues.

« Under the Sink

Storage space can be scarce in a bathroom—so use every square inch you have. This simple storage idea offers a home for hand towels and other bathroom necessities right under the sink.

Antique Modernity ⌄

With some sanding and staining, you can take a vintage wall-hung cabinet like this one, and make a beautiful medicine cabinet for your bathroom. Learn to update other pieces of furniture for bathroom use on pages 94 and 100.

Playtime Caddy ⌃

If you have small kids, establish a little storage station for bath-time toys. Rubber ducks and other squeaky animals make fun design elements.

Smart Shelving »

The problem with store-bought shelving and storage containers: They aren't built to fit your bathroom. With a few simple skills, you can build your own shelves and accessories. See pages 88 and 102 for the lowdown on how to create smart floating box shelves and wood cosmetics boxes like the ones pictured here.

$ $

Bracket shelf with hooks

A clever bracket shelf near your shower or tub adds style and convenience.

Materials

- two 1 x 6 pine boards, each 30 inches long
- wood filler
- primer
- gloss or semi-gloss latex enamel
- two shelf brackets
- four coat hooks with screws

Tools

- sandpaper or sanding sponges, 100 grit, 150 grit, and 180 grit
- microfiber dust cloth and damp cloth
- hammer and nail set
- finish nails, 1½ inch or 2 inch
- wood glue
- paintbrush, ½ inch to ¾ inch (to spread glue)
- putty knife
- drop cloth or newspaper
- synthetic-bristle brush, 1½ inch
- scraps of wood
- tape measure and pencil
- power drill (with bits) and screwdriver
- carpenter's level
- cleat picture hangers, with fasteners (and wall anchors if needed; see step 5)

Steps

1. Prep the wood

With the sandpaper or sanding sponges, smooth both sides of one board (the shelf) and the front of the other board (the ledger), plus all the edges and ends. Start with the coarsest grit and work up to the finest. Wipe off the sawdust with the dust cloth.

2. Assemble the shelf

With the hammer, tap six evenly spaced finish nails into the top of the shelf. Space them evenly ⅜ inch in from the back edge and no closer than 1 inch from each side edge. Drive the nails just far enough so the tips protrude on the back of the board. With the narrower paintbrush, spread glue along the top edge of the ledger. Lower the shelf onto that, lining up the back edges of the shelf and the ledger. Finish driving in the nails. Sink the heads about ⅛ inch using the nail set. Wipe off any glue drips with the damp cloth. Press wood filler into the nail holes with the putty knife. Let dry.

3. Prime and paint

Cover a worktable with a drop cloth or newspaper and place the shelf assembly on it. Sand the wood filler smooth and wipe away the dust with the dust cloth. Coat the top of the shelf with primer, using the wider paintbrush. Then set the back of the ledger on the scraps of wood, and prime the remaining surfaces. Let dry. In the same way, brush enamel over the shelf assembly. Let dry. Apply a second coat if needed.

4. Attach brackets and hooks

Attach the shelf brackets 2 inches from each end, and space the hooks so the first is 6 inches from one end and the other three are 6 inches apart. In each case, mark the screw holes with the pencil, drill pilot holes using a bit slightly thinner than the screws, and screw on the hardware with the screwdriver.

5. Hang the shelf

Locate studs within the wall. Using the drill, screwdriver, and carpenter's level, attach the cleat picture hangers to the studs and to the back of the shelf. If you can't find studs, install wall anchors. (See pages 40–41 for how to find studs and install anchors.) To install the shelf, press it to the wall a little higher than the hangers, then lower it until the hangers slide together.

Style Tip

If you want a look that's a little less industrial, swap out the metal shelf brackets for wooden corbels.

First-Timer Tip

When you're choosing which of the two boards to use as the shelf, select the one with the nicest-looking edge—and face that edge outward.

$

Star-etched ventilated cabinets

Want to add ventilation—and style—to your under-sink vanity? Try this creative solution.

Materials

- primer
- gloss or semi-gloss latex enamel

Tools

- rubber gloves, bucket, and sponge
- household cleaner, or deglosser if existing paint has a gloss finish
- screwdriver
- masking or transparent tape
- graph paper
- ruler and pencil
- glue stick with washable adhesive
- short pieces of 2 by 4s, for spacers
- quick-release bar clamps
- power drill, with ⅜-inch bit
- jigsaw with curve-cutting blade
- small, flat-sided rasp or emery boards
- sandpaper or sanding sponge, 180 grit
- microfiber dust cloth
- drop cloth
- synthetic-bristle brush, 1 inch and 2 inch

▶ Steps

1. Prep

With the screwdriver, take the doors off their hinges and remove the knobs. Wearing gloves, wash the doors with water and the cleaner or deglosser.

2. Create the design

Tape together sheets of graph paper to create two templates, each as big as each vanity door. Decide the size and placement of the stars; stay at least 3 inches from the edges. Using the ruler and pencil, draw several eight-pointed stars on one template in the position you want them. Each star should be two squares set at a 45-degree angle to each other (see illustration). Do the same for the second template, or simply make a photocopy of the first template.

3. Cut out the stars

Most jigsaw blades leave splinters on the side of the wood facing up but not on the back. So, for splinter-free cuts on the front, glue the templates to the back of the doors. On your worktable, set the spacers on their narrow edges, and place one door on top with the template facing up; clamp securely. Drill a small hole through the center of one star drawing. Place the jigsaw blade in the hole, and saw to one point of the star: Begin in a curve but straighten out your cut as you near the point, cutting along the star's outline. Reposition the jigsaw blade in the hole and cut along the opposite side of the point to complete that star point. Continue cutting in the same way until the whole star is cut. Cut the remaining stars in both doors.

4. Smooth the wood

Peel off the remaining graph paper. (Mist the paper with water to soften the glue, if necessary.) Turn the doors right side up. With the rasp or an emery board, smooth the stars' edges. With the sandpaper or sanding sponge, lightly scuff-sand the rest of the door on both sides and on the outside edges. Wipe the surfaces with the dust cloth.

5. Prime and paint

Position the spacer blocks on a drop cloth and place each door face side up on the blocks. Work on one door at a time. With the smaller brush, coat each star's inside edges with primer; with the larger brush, prime the rest of the door front, then the outside edges. Repeat for the other door. Let dry, then flip the doors and brush primer onto the backs of the doors. Let dry. Brush on the latex enamel, using the same process. Let dry.

6. Complete

If the paint looks thin or blotchy when dry, add a second coat. Let dry. Screw the doors back onto the hinges, and reattach the knobs.

Style Note

For a simpler design, cut crescent moons. Or make hearts by drilling pairs of holes, then cutting a point underneath.

First-Timer Tip

Cut a few practice stars on scrap wood that's as similar as possible to the vanity doors.

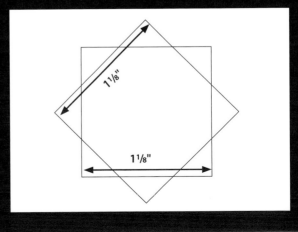

Create the Stars

Each star consists of two squares set at a 45-degree angle to each other. To make cutouts like those in the photo, start with squares 1⅛ inch on each side; this results in stars 1½ inches tall.

Ⓢ

Floating box shelves

Need more storage in your bathroom? Wooden wall-mounted box shelves are a quick and clever solution.

Materials

(for one box; adapt as needed)

- 1 x 8 pine board, 2 feet long (for the back)
- 1 x 6 pine board, 5 feet long (for the top, bottom, and ends)
- wipe-on water-based finish

Tools

- tape measure and pencil
- combination square
- jigsaw or handsaw
- sandpaper or sanding sponges, 100 grit, 150 grit, and 180 grit
- hammer
- finish nails, 1¾ or 2 inch
- wood glue
- paintbrush, ½ inch to ¾ inch (to spread glue)
- damp cloth
- microfiber dust cloth
- cloth or foam brush (to apply finish)
- power drill (with bits) and screwdriver
- cleat picture hangers, with fasteners (and wall anchors if needed; see step 6)
- carpenter's level

▶Steps

1. Cut the pieces

Using the tape measure, pencil, and combination square, mark off 24 inches at each end of the 1 x 6 pine board. With the jigsaw or handsaw, cut out the pieces. These are the top and bottom parts of the box shelf. Then, from the same board, mark and cut a piece at each end that is 5¾ inches long. Leave the shorter board as is, for the back.

2. Sand the wood

With the sandpaper or sanding sponges, smooth any rough spots. Start with the coarsest grit and work up to the finest. For now, avoid rounding over the corners along the edges.

3. Assemble the top and bottom

With the hammer, tap finish nails into the outside face of the top and bottom pieces, one nail near each corner. Place each nail ⅜ inch in from the narrow end and 1 inch away from the long edge. Tap in all eight nails just far enough for the tips to protrude on the other side of the board. With the paintbrush, apply glue to the cut edge of one of the side pieces. Align the glued area with the top piece, and tap in the nails a bit to lock in the position. Repeat with the other end piece. Rotate the assembly so the top faces up. Hammer in the nails. Rotate the pieces so the top faces down. Brush glue on the edges that are facing up. Then position the bottom piece, and hammer in the nails.

4. Add the back

Place the partially assembled box with its front edges facing down. Brush glue around the edges that will sit against the back of the box. Lower the back piece into place, and drive in 16 nails (2 on each end, 6 on each side) around the perimeter to secure it (see illustration). Keep the nails ⅜ inch from edges and at least 1 inch from the corners. Wipe off any glue drips with the damp cloth. Let the glue dry.

5. Finish the box

Do any touch-up sanding, including rounding over the exposed edges. Wipe off the sawdust with the dust cloth. Apply the finish as the manufacturer recommends. Let dry.

6. Hang the shelf or shelves

Locate studs within the wall. Using the drill, screwdriver, and carpenter's level, attach the cleat picture hangers to the studs and to the back of the shelf. If you can't find studs, use wall anchors instead. (See pages 40–41 for how to find studs and install anchors.) To install the shelf, press it to the wall a little higher than the hangers, then lower it until the hangers slide together.

First-Timer Tip
Orient all pieces so the wood's growth rings curve in toward the center of the box. That way, when the wood cups (bends) as it absorbs shower moisture, the joints in the box will stay tight.

Assemble the box

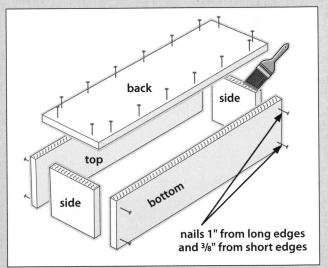

nails 1" from long edges and ⅜" from short edges

Following steps 3 and 4, assemble the box shelf using nails and glue.

$

Doorless cabinet

If the door to your bathroom cabinet is creaky, peeling, or simply gets in the way, be bold and remove it! For a finished look, you'll want it to seem like it was never there.

Materials
- wood filler
- primer
- gloss or semi-gloss latex enamel, 1 quart

Tools
- drop cloths
- scraps of wood (to support shelves while paint dries, if shelves need to be painted)
- screwdriver
- rubber gloves, bucket, and sponge
- household cleaner, or deglosser if existing paint has a gloss finish
- putty knife
- sandpaper or sanding sponge, 180 grit
- microfiber dust cloth
- painter's masking tape, 1 inch or wider
- synthetic-bristle brush, 1 inch to 2 inch

Steps

1. Prep the shelves and door
Take out all removable shelves. If they are glass (as pictured here), set them and the shelf supports aside. If the shelves are wood and need painting, cover a worktable with a drop cloth, arrange the wood scraps, and set the shelves on top of them. With the screwdriver, remove the screws holding the door hinges to the cabinet. Use the putty knife to press wood filler into the screw holes and any hinge recesses cut into the cabinet. Fill deep recesses in thin layers, allowing each layer to dry before you add the next. Let dry.

2. Wash and scuff
Wearing gloves, wash the cabinet interior and the surrounding trim with water and the cleaner or deglosser. Also wash the shelves if you plan to repaint them or just want to clean them. (Avoid using deglosser on glass shelves; it might etch them.) Let the surfaces dry, and then use the sandpaper or sanding sponge to lightly scuff up all the areas you plan to repaint. Do not sand through the paint. Wipe the surfaces with the dust cloth.

3. Tape
Apply painter's masking tape to the wall just beyond the cabinet trim. Press down firmly on the tape edges that face the trim.

4. Prime
With the brush, apply primer to the patched areas. Or prime everything (the shelves, the entire cabinet interior, and the surrounding trim) if you are dramatically changing the color or are switching from oil paint to latex. (To learn how to test if old paint is oil based, see page 33.) If you are priming everything, use the procedure recommended for painting in step 5.

5. Paint and complete
If you are painting the shelves, paint one side and the front edge and let dry. On the cabinet, work from the interior out, and do the trim last. As you complete each section, make a series of parallel long passes to smooth the paint. Let dry. Flip the shelves and paint the other side. Let dry. Inspect the finish. If the paint looks thin or blotchy, add a second coat. Let that dry, and reinstall the shelves.

First-Timer Tip

If screw recesses are caked with multiple layers of paint, and the screwdriver tip won't fit in the screw, use a utility knife to pare away some of the dried paint.

Style Notes

>> Now that the inside of your medicine cabinet is in full view, dress it up a little. Line the shelves with paper that's a few inches wider than the shelves, and cut a pretty scallop pattern to fold over the front edges.

>> Transfer the contents of plastic containers to attractive glass jars to make toiletries look and feel more organized.

$

Cabinet with curtain

Add a curtain with a lively print to your built-in vanity or bathroom shelving to hide unstylish bottles and toiletries—and add a bit of flair.

Materials
- fiberglass rod, 3/8 inch by width of cabinet opening
- fabric (see step 2 for yardage)
- pompom fringe (see step 4 for yardage)

Tools
- pencil
- tape measure
- power drill with bits
- screwdriver
- two threaded inserts, No. 8-32
- two eye bolts, No. 8-32, 1 5/8 inches long
- hacksaw with fine-tooth blade
- two cup hooks, 1 1/8 inches long
- yardstick and carpenter's square
- scissors
- iron, and ironing pad or ironing board
- sewing machine or needle
- thread
- sewing pins

Steps

1. Prep the rod
With the pencil and tape measure, mark the cabinet side walls where you want to affix the curtain rod (at least 1/2 inch from the top of the space and 1 inch in from the front edge). At each mark, use a 1/4-inch drill bit to drill a hole 1/2 inch deep. With the screwdriver, twist the threaded inserts into the holes. Then screw in the eye bolts. With the hacksaw, cut the rod to the length between the eye bolts, minus 1 inch. In each end of the rod, drill a hole slightly smaller than the shaft of the cup hooks. Twist in the cup hooks.

2. Measure and cut the fabric
Measure the width of the opening and the distance from the bottom edge of the cabinet to the top edge of the cup hooks. Then, to find the fabric width, multiply the width of the opening by 1 1/2 (for fullness) and add 4 inches (for the side hems). To find the fabric length, add the height you measured plus 9 inches (for the rod pocket at the top and the hem at the bottom). With the yardstick, carpenter's square, and pencil, mark the fabric to match these dimensions. Cut out the fabric with the scissors.

3. Hem the edges
Place the fabric wrong side up on the ironing pad or ironing board. Turn up 1 inch along both sides, then fold those over again and press flat, creating double hems. With the sewing machine or the needle and thread, stitch the hems. In a similar way, create a double hem at the bottom, but make these folds 3 inches wide. Along the top edge, create the rod pocket by making a double hem that's 1 1/2 inches deep.

4. Add the fringe
Cut the pompom fringe to the finished width of the curtain plus 1 inch. Fold over and pin back 1/2 inch of the trim at each end. Using the yardstick, draw a line across the fabric where you want the top edge of the trim. Pin the trim to the fabric using the straight pins. Sew the trim in place.

5. Hang the curtain
Thread the rod into the rod pocket. Slip the cup hooks at the ends of the rod into the eye screws in the cabinet.

First-Timer Tip

Fiberglass rods, like the one indicated for this project, can be found at stores that sell plastics and in kite-building kits.

Alternate Method

You can also hang the curtain from a cafe curtain tension rod. This kind of rod stays in place on its own—no drilling necessary.

($)

Refinished tray and stand

Display towels or toiletries in an elegant way by freshening up a secondhand wood tray on a stand with a little paint. Use anything from a butler's tray to a TV stand.

Materials

(not including tray and stand)

- wood filler
- primer
- semi-gloss or gloss latex enamel, 1 quart

Tools

- drop cloth or newspaper
- spacer blocks
- screwdriver (if tray or stand has removable hardware)
- painter's masking tape, any width
- putty knife
- sandpaper or sanding sponges, 100 grit and 180 grit
- microfiber dust cloth
- paint tray
- mini roller
- synthetic-bristle brush, 1 inch or 1½ inch

Steps

1. Prep

Position the drop cloth or newspaper. With the screwdriver, remove any hardware that is screwed on, such as the brass corner brackets found on some butler's trays. Protect any other hardware, such as pivot pins on the stand, by covering the metal with painter's masking tape. Press down on all tape edges that face areas you will paint.

2. Smooth out the surfaces

Place the tray and stand on spacer blocks. With wood filler and the putty knife, fill in any cracks and gaps. Let dry, and then sand the filled patches with the 100-grit sandpaper or sanding sponge. Scuff-sand all surfaces with the 180-grit sandpaper or sanding sponge. Wipe the surface with the dust cloth.

3. Prime and paint

Set the tray right side up on the spacer blocks. Pour the primer into the tray. With the roller, prime all visible surfaces on the stand and the tray. As you prime each area, immediately follow up with the brush to remove any drips. Brush with long strokes in the direction of the wood grain. Then use the same procedure to paint the stand and the tray. When the paint is dry, add a second coat. Let dry. Reattach any hardware you removed.

($)

Sink skirt

Whether it's frilly or just plain fun, a fabric skirt is a great way to dress up a wall-mounted sink. Bonus: It also creates a practical place for bathroom storage by letting you hide toiletries and other bathroom essentials underneath.

Materials
- main skirt fabric (for yardage, see step 1)
- contrasting fabric, 1 yard
- corded piping trim
- hook-and-loop tape with sew-on and self-stick sides

Tools
- tape measure
- pencil and yardstick (to measure fabric)
- scissors
- iron, and ironing pad or ironing board
- thread
- sewing machine
- sewing pins

Style Note
Use vibrant fabric if you want to call attention to the sink, or more neutral fabric if you want other bathroom features to stand out.

Steps

1. Cut the fabric
Measure the three exposed sides of the sink perimeter and multiply by 1½. That will be the horizontal dimension of the main fabric. Then measure the height you want for the total skirt length, and subtract 6 inches for the contrasting bands and their seams. Cut the main fabric to these dimensions. From the contrasting fabric, cut four strips 8 inches wide—three strips as long as the skirt perimeter and one strip an inch longer.

2. Create the bottom band
Sew the three same-length contrasting strips end to end, with right sides facing together and ½-inch-wide seams. Near each end of the resulting long strip, fold the fabric lengthwise with the right side in and sew across the band ½ inch from the short edges (see illustration below). Turn the fabric right side out. Fold the entire strip lengthwise and iron it flat.

3. Create the top band
Take the strip of contrasting fabric with the extra inch and iron it in half lengthwise, right side out, creating a crease. Open up the fabric and place it right side up. Sew the sew-on part of the hook-and-loop tape alongside the crease, to a single layer of fabric (see illustration on next page), stopping the tape ½ inch from each short edge. Fold the fabric so that the right side faces in. Sew across the fabric ½ inch from each short edge. Turn the fabric right side out and again fold it lengthwise. Iron it flat.

continued on next page

Create the bottom band

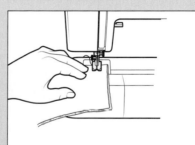

Sew ½ inch from the short edges, with right sides facing each other.

4. Hem the sides of the skirt

On each side edge of the main fabric, fold ½ inch to the back, then fold that over a second time, creating a double hem. Iron it flat, and sew the hem.

5. Create the gathers

Adjust the machine to its longest straight stitch. On the longer contrasting strip, sew lengthwise through both layers in two parallel lines, ½ inch and ⅜ inch from the cut edge. Pull on the bobbin threads to create gathers until the strip is short enough to match the bottom edge of the main fabric (see illustration). Then gather the top edge of the main fabric until it is as short as the top contrasting band.

6. Add the corded piping

On the right side of the fabric, sew the corded piping to the bottom edge of the main fabric and to the side of the top contrasting band that doesn't have hook-and-loop tape. In both cases, face the corded part of the piping away from the edge and stitch along the cord (see illustration). At the ends, turn the piping into the seam allowance.

7. Sew the bands to the skirt

At the bottom of the skirt, place the gathered edge band over the corded piping, overlapping all the raw edges. Pin in place, then flip over the layers so you can see the stitches from step 6. Sew over those, through all the layers, removing the pins as you go. Join the gathered top edge of the skirt to the top band in the same way.

8. Hang the skirt

Press the adhesive-backed hook-and-loop tape onto the sink perimeter and attach the skirt.

Style Note

For the skirt and ruffle, pair a pretty print with stripes that pick up the same colors (as pictured here), or mix polka dots and a plaid.

Create the top band

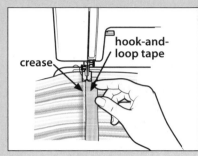

Starting ½ inch from the edge and leaving a ½-inch allowance, sew the hook-and-loop tape at one side of the crease.

Create the gathers

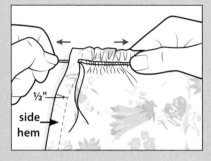

Pull on the bobbin threads to create gathers.

Add the corded piping

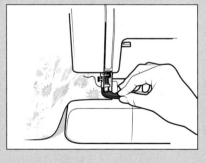

Face the corded side of the piping away from the raw edge of the fabric and stitch along the cord. Turn the piping into the seam allowance.

Alternate Method

For a no-sew alternative, start with a curtain that's gathered on the top. Adjust the length by affixing iron-on hemming tape to the bottom edge.

First-Timer Tip

Leave the skirt in place for at least 24 hours while the hook-and-loop adhesive reaches full strength. After that, you can remove the skirt for laundering, as needed.

($) ($)

Wood-framed mirror shelf

A simple wood-framed mirror shelf lets you cross two things off your bathroom wish list: a convenient mirror over the sink and a handy shelf for toiletries.

Materials

- 1 x 6 pine board, 9 feet long
- ¾-inch plywood, cut to 2 feet by 2 feet
- glass mirror, cut to ¼ inch by 2 feet by 2 feet
- wipe-on, water-based finish

Tools

- tape measure and pencil
- combination square
- jigsaw or handsaw
- sandpaper or sanding sponges, 100 grit, 150 grit, and 180 grit
- hammer
- finish nails, 2¼ inch
- wood glue and paintbrush (to spread glue)
- microfiber dust cloth
- mirror adhesive with caulk gun
- power drill, with bits
- screwdriver
- carpenter's level
- cleat picture hangers, with fasteners (and wall anchors if needed; see step 6)

Style Note

Dress up the mirror with a stenciled design, like a Celtic knot in each corner or a delicate vine border. Instead of paint, use etching cream (available at craft-supply stores) to create a more translucent effect.

▶ Steps

1. Cut the frame

Using the tape measure, pencil, and combination square, mark 24 inches from one end of the pine board. With the jigsaw or handsaw, cut out the piece. This is the bottom of the shelf. Then, from the same board, mark and cut a piece at each end that is 24¾ inches long. These are the sides. Finally, cut a piece 25½ inches long, for the top.

2. Sand the wood

With the sandpaper or sanding sponges, smooth any rough spots. Start with the coarsest grit and work up to the finest. Don't round over the corners just yet.

3. Attach the sides to the bottom

With the hammer, tap two finish nails into the outside face of each frame side, ⅜ inch from the bottom, 1 inch from the front and 1 inch from the back. Hammer just until the nail tips protrude on the other side. With the paintbrush, apply glue to one of the cut ends of the frame bottom. Align the glued area with the inside face of one frame side, where the nails are protruding. Tap in the nails a bit to lock in the position. Rotate the assembly so the side is on top. Hammer in the nails. Attach the other side to the bottom the same way.

4. Add the top

Tap two finish nails into each end of the outside face of the top piece, ⅜ inch from one end, 1 inch from the front and 1 inch from the back. Then, 3 inches from each end, start two nails ⅜ inch from the back edge (these will nail into the plywood). Tip the frame so it rests on its bottom, and spread glue on the top edges of both frame sides. Align the top, and hammer in the 4 nails at the edges. Place the frame face up on your workbench. Lower the plywood into the box. Tap in those nails. Then, rotating the frame as needed, continue to nail in the plywood all the way around, using a total of four nails per side.

5. Finish the frame

Do any touch-up sanding, including rounding over the front edges. Wipe off the sawdust with the dust cloth. Apply the finish as the manufacturer recommends. Let dry.

6. Add the mirror and hang

Using the caulk gun, spread mirror adhesive on the plywood or the back of the mirror, as recommended on the adhesive label. Lower the mirror into place, and press down firmly to spread the adhesive. Let dry for at least two days. Locate studs within the wall. Using the drill, screwdriver, and carpenter's level, attach the cleat picture hangers to the studs and to the back of the plywood. If you can't find studs, install wall anchors. (See pages 40–41 for how to find studs and install anchors.) Hang the frame.

(See pages 40–41 for how to find studs and install anchors.)

First-Timer Tip

Before you cut the frame, set the mirror on the plywood, and measure the outside edges. If any side exceeds 24 inches, or if the mirror extends past the plywood, increase all the frame pieces by the extra amount.

Attach the plywood

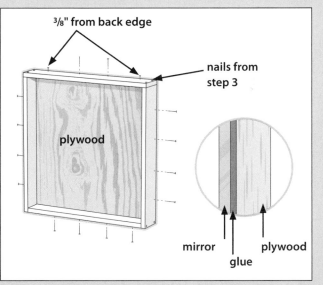

³⁄₈" from back edge

nails from step 3

plywood

mirror   plywood

glue

Lower the plywood into the box so the back edges of the frame and plywood line up. Tap in the two nails on the top frame piece that are ⅜ inches from the back edge. In a similar way, nail in the plywood all the way around.

$

Refinished hutch

An updated hutch is perfect for a bathroom. In the glass cabinet, display collectibles and elegant containers of toiletries. In the drawers, hide everything else!

Materials
(not including hutch)
- wood filler (if wood needs patching)
- primer
- semi-gloss latex enamel (for interior), 1 quart
- gloss or semi-gloss latex enamel (for exterior), 1 quart

Tools
- pencil
- screwdriver
- drop cloths or newspaper
- spacer blocks (to support doors and shelves while you paint them)
- putty knife (to apply wood filler)
- sandpaper or sanding sponge, 180 grit (plus coarser grits if surface is rough)
- microfiber dust cloth
- painter's masking tape, any width
- paint tray
- mini roller
- synthetic-bristle brush, 1 inch or 1½ inch

Steps

1. Take it apart
Remove the drawers and any moveable shelves, and use the pencil to number each one on the back to identify where it fits. Use the screwdriver to remove the hinges, and take off the doors. Also remove handles or knobs on the drawers and doors. Set the hardware aside. Place the hutch on the drop cloth or newspaper, and set the doors and shelves on spacer blocks that are positioned on other drop cloths.

2. Smooth out the surfaces
With wood filler and the putty knife, fill any cracks and gaps. Once the filler is dry, lightly sand all the surfaces with the 180-grit sandpaper or sanding sponge. (If the surface is rough, start with 80 to 100 grit, proceed to 120 to 150 grit, and finish with 180 grit.) Wipe the surfaces with the dust cloth.

3. Tape
Apply the painter's masking tape to the glass next to the door frames. Press down firmly on the tape edges that face the wood.

4. Prime
Pour some primer into the tray. With the roller, prime all visible surfaces on the hutch, starting with the interior and working out. Also prime the drawer fronts and outside edges, and the top surfaces and front edges of the shelves. As you prime each area, immediately follow up with the brush to remove any excess drips of primer. Brush with long strokes in the direction of the wood grain. The door frames are narrow, so switch to using the brush alone to prime them on one side and along the edges. Let dry. Then tip over the doors and shelves and prime the backs. Let dry.

5. Paint and complete
Pour some of the enamel for the interior into the tray. Paint the hutch interior and shelves, following the procedure from step 4. Coat the remaining surfaces with the enamel for the exterior. Let dry. Add a second coat (you can skip this on the underside of the shelves if you want). Let dry, then remove the tape on the doors. Reassemble the hutch.

Style Note
To create a more attractive display, transfer toiletries like cotton balls and hairpins to beautiful boxes or jars with colorful lids that match the cabinet exterior.

First-Timer Tip
Before you take apart the hutch, make sure the drawers and doors open and close properly. Do any necessary repairs to the hutch, including scraping off globs of old paint, before proceeding with the project.

($)

Cosmetics boxes

Why buy pricey storage containers for cosmetics and other bathroom essentials when you can easily make your own, complete with dividers in exactly the places you want them?

Materials

- ¼ x 8 poplar board, 12 inches long (for the bottom)
- two ¼ x 3 poplar boards, 30 inches long (for the sides, ends, and dividers)
- wipe-on water-based finish

Tools

- tape measure
- pencil
- combination square
- jigsaw, or miter box with backsaw
- sandpaper or sanding sponge, 180 grit
- microfiber dust cloth
- cloth or foam brush (to apply finish)
- wire brads, ¾ inch by 20 gauge
- hammer
- wood glue
- artist's brush (to spread glue)
- damp cloth

▶Steps

1. Cut the pieces

Using the tape measure, pencil, and combination square, mark off 12 inches at each end of one ¼ x 3 poplar board. With the jigsaw or backsaw, cut out the pieces. These will be the sides of the box. Then, from the second board, mark and cut a piece at each end that is 6¾ inches long. These will be the ends. From the same board, mark and cut another pair of pieces 6¾ inches long, for the dividers. Leave the ¼ x 8 poplar board as is, for the bottom.

2. Sand and finish the wood

With the sandpaper, smooth any splinters left from the saw. Avoid rounding over the edges. Wipe off the sawdust with the dust cloth. Apply the finish as the manufacturer recommends. Let dry.

3. Prep the sides

On the bottom edge of each side piece, label the left end (just pick one end as "left") in pencil. Using the combination square, mark pairs of dots that are ⅜ inch from the long edges and ⅛ inch, 4 inches, 8 inches and 11⅞ inches from the left end. Start wire brads at all the marks, hammering the brads just far enough so the tips protrude on the back of the boards.

4. Attach the ends and dividers

With the brush, apply glue to one end of each end piece. Align one end to one side, and tap in the brads a bit more to lock in the position. Set the other end piece in the same way. Then rotate the assembly so the side piece is on top. Hammer in the brads. Repeat for each divider. Rotate the assembly so the nailed side faces down. Brush glue on the other ends of the dividers and the ends, set the remaining side piece on top, and drive in the brads.

5. Add the bottom

Place the partially assembled box upside down. Brush glue around the edges that will sit against the bottom. Lower the bottom piece into place, and drive in 10 brads (3 on each end, 2 on each side) around the perimeter to secure it (see illustration). Keep the brads ⅛ inch in from edges and ⅜ inch from the corners. Wipe off glue drips with the damp cloth. Let dry.

Style Note

To protect the wood and save yourself from dusting tight corners, line the bottom of each cubbyhole with small cut-to-fit pieces of fabric. When they get grimy, simply replace them.

First-Timer Tips

» Home centers carry thin "project wood" that's perfect for making these boxes and the dividers. The boards come flat and sanded, saving you prep time. Poplar is a better choice than maple or oak.

» If you want to make additional dividers, assemble the innermost sections first, so there's space to swing the hammer. And use T intersections; X crossings are impossible to nail.

Assemble the box

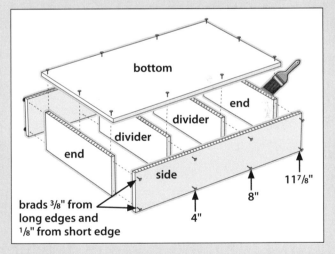

Following steps 3–5, assemble the box using brads and glue.

5

Accessorize with style

No bathroom is complete without the right accessories. And although you could purchase your bath accessories at a department store, making your own is so much more rewarding. Want to learn how to create candle ledges above your bath? Sew your own faux Roman shades? Or frame a mirror with natural stone? This chapter will show you how. And the best part about creating your own accessories is that you can adapt them in ways that will best fit the needs of your home—and the people who live in it.

Adaptable Mirrors ⩔

No need to lean in to the sink to see yourself in the mirror. Install extension mirrors, and pull the mirrors out to you! For more creative mirror ideas, see the stone-framed mirror (page 126), the mirror mosaic (page 122), and the mirror on a cord (page 118).

Modern Shades ⩓

Circular designs, like the one on this roller shade, add a sense of motion to your space. Patterned roller shades are perfect coverings for bathroom windows because they let in light but still offer needed privacy. You can also draw a stencil on your roller shade—see page 142 to learn how.

⩕ Purple by Design

With a few simple wall hooks and a handful of colorful towels, you can change the look and feel of your bathroom. Drape a sixth towel over the tub, or throw in a matching bath mat to complete the look. For more towel hook ideas, see pages 114 and 116.

A Touch of ⚡ Antiquity

An electric candelabra like this one has a lovely, old-fashioned feel, especially when you match it with a simple dark tray that holds a bowl of delicate hand soaps.

Anagrammed Hooks »

Whose towel is whose? You'll never have to wonder again if you put everyone's initial atop their personal towel hook. Another take on the idea: use icons instead, like a star, baseball, heart, guitar, or paintbrush.

Lights, Shower Curtain, Action! »

Create a lively look in your bathroom by installing a band of lights above the sink and adding a shower curtain with a design in a color that really pops—like bright red. For added style, paint the trim the same vibrant color.

($)

Shower hooks

No place to hang bath sponges, wash-cloths, or towels in your tile shower? A couple of hooks make a huge difference. Here's how to get the job done efficiently—without breaking the tile.

Materials
- three double hooks, with screws

Tools
- masking tape
- tape measure
- pencil
- carpenter's level
- power drill, with standard bits
- ¼-inch specialty bit for glass and tile
- spray bottle with water
- plastic expansion anchors, ¼ inch diameter
- hammer
- screwdriver

Alternate Method
If you want to hang a complete caddy from your shower wall, install a stainless steel or ceramic knob (instead of the shower hooks) at the far end of the shower. Voila!—instant extra storage.

Steps

1. Mark the hook locations
Decide approximately where you want your hooks and cover the general area with masking tape. If you want the hooks to be evenly spaced (as pictured here), use the tape measure and pencil to mark the bottom edge of the desired hook locations on the masking tape. Then, using the carpenter's level, draw a horizontal line across the tape where the marks are. Make a mark on the masking tape where the left edge of each hook will be. Make sure that all screw holes will be over tile, not grout lines. When the locations are aligned, mark the screw holes with the pencil.

2. Drill
With the drill set to a low speed, place the tip of the bit firmly against the tape at one of the screw marks, and begin drilling. It's best if you can have a helper lightly mist the tile with the spray bottle as you drill, so the bit doesn't overheat. If you must work solo, stop drilling frequently to mist and let the bit cool. If you are using a carbide bit, drill with it perpendicular to the wall. If you are using a diamond bit, start at an angle and straighten out once the tip has penetrated the tile surface. In either case, the tape should help the bit dig in where you want it to rather than skate across the tile. Maintain steady pressure on the drill, but do not press in so much that you force the bit. Drill until the bit breaks into a hollow space behind the wall or hits wood. Repeat for all screw holes. Remove the tape.

3. Finish the holes and insert the anchors
At any hole where the bit hit wood, switch to a standard bit to finish drilling a pilot hole. Use a bit that is slightly smaller than the screws. At each hole where the wall is hollow, press a plastic expansion anchor into place. Tap the anchor with the hammer until the front of the anchor is flush with the tile.

4. Attach the hooks
Using the screwdriver, insert the screws to attach the hooks to the wall.

First-Timer Tip

When you are installing the hooks, stop turning as soon as the screws are tight. Overtightening doesn't make the hooks more secure and, if you are using anchors, over-tightening can strip the threads, causing the screws to pull loose.

($)

Candle ledges

Build these lovely candle ledges to keep your candle flames away from splashes.

Materials

(for one pair of ledges; adapt as needed)

- 1 x 6 pine board, 12 inches long (for platforms)

- 1 x 3 pine board, 12 inches long (for backs)

- skewback or solid crown molding, 1½ inches high and wide, 12 inches long (for bracing)

- primer

- gloss or semi-gloss latex paint

Tools

- tape measure and pencil

- combination square

- jigsaw, or a miter box with handsaw

- sandpaper or sanding sponge, 180 grit

- microfiber dust cloth

- hammer and finish nails, 1¾ inch

- wood glue

- paintbrush (to spread glue)

- drop cloth or newspaper and spacer blocks

- synthetic-bristle brush, 1 inch or 1½ inch

- power drill (with bits) and screwdriver

- carpenter's level

- cleat picture hangers, with fasteners (and wall anchors if needed; see step 6)

▶ Steps

1. Cut the pieces

Using the tape measure, pencil, and combination square, mark 5½ inches from one end of each board. Also mark 4 inches from one end of the molding. With the jigsaw or handsaw, cut out the pieces. Measure, mark, and cut identical sets of parts for as many additional ledges as you want.

2. Sand the wood

With the sandpaper or sanding sponge, smooth any splinters, but don't round the edges. Wipe clean with the dust cloth.

3. Assemble the platforms and backs

With the hammer, tap two finish nails into the top of each platform piece, near the back. Place each nail ⅜ inch from the long edge and 1 inch from the narrow end. Tap in the nails just far enough for the tips to protrude on the other side. With the paintbrush, apply glue to the top edge of one back piece. Align the glued area under the nails in the top piece, lining up the back surfaces. Hammer in the nails. Repeat for the other ledges.

4. Add the bracing

Measure in ¾ inch from each end of the back piece, underneath the platform, and make a pencil mark. Brush glue onto the back and top surfaces of a molding piece. Press the piece into place against the top and back, centered between the pencil lines, and hold it for a few minutes. Repeat for the other ledges. Let dry.

5. Prime and paint

Position the drop cloth or newspaper, and place the ledges, wall side down, on the spacer blocks. With the brush, apply primer to all the visible surfaces, taking care not to leave any drips. Brush with long strokes in the direction of the wood grain. Let dry. Brush on the paint, using the same procedure. Let dry. Apply a second coat, and let dry.

6. Mount

Decide how you want to arrange the ledges on the wall. Identify which locations have studs behind them. Using the drill, screwdriver, and carpenter's level, attach the cleat picture hangers to the studs and to the backs of the ledges. If you can't find studs, use wall anchors instead. (See pages 40–41 for how to find studs and install anchors.) Hang the shelves.

Style Note

Use gloss paint for the ledges; the shiny surface reflects light well, adding to the glow of the candlelight.

Alternate Method

If you have tiled walls above the bathtub, attach the ledges with removable mounting tape strong enough to hold several pounds, or drill through the tile as if you were installing hooks on tile (see page 110).

Assemble the ledge

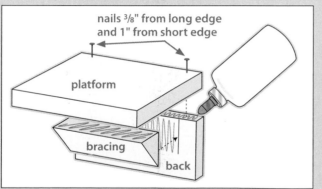

nails ⅜" from long edge and 1" from short edge

platform

bracing

back

Attach the platform to the back (step 3), and then glue the bracing to the underside of the ledge (step 4). Hold the bracing for a few minutes to let the glue set.

$

Wood knob towel hooks

Towel hooks keep the bathroom tidy, but that doesn't mean they have to look utilitarian. Create your own towel hooks with beautiful round wood knobs to give your bathroom a stylish, organic feel.

Materials
- 5 wood knobs of varying sizes

Tools
- pencil
- power drill with bits
- locking pliers
- 5 dowel screws, 2 inch or 2½ inch, with a diameter that fits knobs
- screw-in wall anchors (if needed; see steps 2 and 4)

Alternate Method
Instead of relying on wall anchors to hold the knobs where the wall is hollow, screw all the knobs to a board or piece of plywood. Then attach to the wall with a couple of nails or screws where there is framing underneath.

Steps

1. Design the layout
Decide where you want the knobs, and mark the locations on the wall with the pencil. For the best air circulation (so the towels dry quickly), space the knobs at least 5 inches apart; also, position them at least 4 feet high so the towels won't touch the floor.

2. Drill the holes
With the drill outfitted with a ⅛-inch-diameter bit, drill a hole at each spot where you want a knob. If the bit hits a hollow cavity (typically about ½ inch in), switch the drill to reverse and extract the bit. If you hit wood framing, drill deeper, a total of 1½ to 2 inches deep. If some knob locations are hollow and others have framing behind them, mark the hollow ones. Re-drill at the hollow locations using a larger bit sized to the outside diameter of the screw-in wall anchors.

3. Prep the knobs
Attach a dowel screw to the hole on the back of each knob. Use the locking pliers to grip the smooth section in the middle of the screw (or, if there is no smooth section, grip the threads ¾ inch from the tip). Turn the pliers clockwise to secure the screw to the knob.

4. Attach the knobs
At each hole where the wall is hollow, screw in an anchor until it is flush with the wall. Screw one of the prepared knobs into the anchor, tightening it just until the back of the knob is flush with the wall. At each hole where you hit wood framing, screw in a prepared knob, tightening only until the back of the knob is flush with the wall.

Style Note
To make your knob-style towel holders look even more interesting, use varying sizes. Another idea: Use Craftsman-style pyramid knobs or finials designed for drapery rod ends; the latter often come already outfitted with dowel screws.

First-Timer Tip
Don't know where to find wood knobs? Try your local lumberyard or hardware store or, for really big knobs, a woodworking supply store.

$

Wooden hook rail

If your family uses a lot of towels, install a classic wood rail with coat hangers. It will keep order in the bathroom by giving each towel a home.

Materials

- 1 x 4 pine board (see steps 1 and 2 to determine the length)
- coat hooks (with a base plate no more than 3 inches long), with screws
- wipe-on water-based finish

Tools

- tape measure
- masking tape
- carpenter's level
- pencil
- combination square
- handsaw or jigsaw
- sandpaper or sanding sponges, 100 grit, 150 grit, and 180 grit
- microfiber dust cloth
- power drill with bits
- screwdriver
- two or more nails with heads, 3 inch
- hammer
- picture hanger hooks, with ⅝-inch-long screws

▶ Steps

1. Design the layout

Decide where you want to hang the rail and how many hooks you want on it. (For the best air circulation, so the towels dry quickly, space the hooks at least 5 inches apart, and plan to hang the rail at least 4 feet high to prevent the towels from dragging on the floor.) Next, locate the studs within the wall (see page 40 to learn how). Adjust the desired location of the rail to accommodate the location of the studs (the rail can extend past each support stud by a foot if needed). With the masking tape, mark each stud where you will hang the rail. Use the carpenter's level to make sure the marks line up horizontally.

2. Cut the rail

With the tape measure and pencil, mark the board for length. At the mark, trace against the combination square to make a line perpendicular to the board's long edge. Saw just beyond the line.

3. Sand and finish the rail

With the sandpaper or sanding sponges, smooth the rail's front face and its top and bottom edges, and round over the corners that will face out. Start with the coarsest grit and work up to the finest. Wipe all the surfaces with the dust cloth. Apply the finish as the manufacturer recommends. Let dry.

4. Attach the hooks

Place the rail face up on a worktable and space the hooks evenly. Mark the screw holes with the pencil. Drill pilot holes using a bit slightly smaller than the screws, and insert the screws with the screwdriver.

5. Drive the nails

At each place you marked on the wall in step 1, hammer in one nail. Leave at least ½ inch of the nail exposed. (If the walls are plaster, drill pilot holes first so you don't crack the plaster.)

6. Hang the rail

Put small pieces of masking tape along the top edge of the rail corresponding to the nail locations on the wall. At each piece of tape, align a picture hanger on the back of the rail so that the part that hooks over a nail projects above the rail. Mark the screw locations for the hangers, and drill pilot holes slightly smaller than the shafts of the screws. With the screwdriver, attach the hangers. Hang the rail on the nails.

Style Note

Choose wood and hooks that complement your decor. An oak rail and antiqued-brass hooks, pictured here, are a classic style. For a more elegant look, use poplar stained with a mahogany finish and shiny brass hooks, or pair black-stained wood with pewter.

First-Timer Tip

To space the hooks evenly, subtract the offset you want at the ends from the total rail length. Divide that distance by the total number of hooks plus 1. That's the interval between hooks.

$ $

Mirror with decorative cord

No vanity over your sink? You can still hang a mirror by mounting a pine board to the wall and adding a decorative strap. The best part: You can hang the mirror at any height you like.

Materials

- one 1 x 6 pine (or other wood) board, 2 feet long
- wipe-on water-based finish
- knob with 1-inch machine screw
- round mirror with wood frame
- decorative cord

Tools

- tape measure
- pencil
- straightedge
- handsaw or jigsaw
- sandpaper or sanding sponges, 100 grit, 150 grit, and 180 grit
- microfiber dust cloth
- power drill (with bits) and screwdriver
- wood screws, 2½ inch or 3 inch
- carpenter's level
- two eye screws (with eyes that the decorative cord fits through)
- screwdriver (optional)
- scissors

▸Steps

1. Shape the mounting board

On the front of the board, use the tape measure and pencil to mark 1½ inches in both directions from each corner. With the straightedge, draw a diagonal line connecting the marks near each corner. With the handsaw or jigsaw, cut just outside the lines.

2. Sand and finish the board

With the sandpaper or sanding sponges, smooth any rough spots. Start with the coarsest grit and work up to the finest. Round over the outside edges. Wipe all the surfaces with the dust cloth. Rub on the finish as the manufacturer recommends. Let dry.

3. Complete the board

With the tape measure and pencil, mark the board 12 inches from one short edge and 1¾ inches from the top edge. There, drill a hole that's the same diameter as the machine screw all the way through the board. From the back, insert the screw into the hole; then on the front of the board, twist on the knob. Tighten the knob by holding the screw head in place with the screwdriver.

4. Hang the board

Locate the studs within the wall near where you want to hang the mirror (see page 40 to learn how). You'll know when you've hit a stud when you hear a hollow sound change to a thud. Once you locate two studs, drill pilot holes into the studs, using a bit slightly smaller than the wood screws (see Alternate Method if you can't locate studs). Use the carpenter's level to make sure the board is straight before you drill the second pilot hole.

5. Prep the mirror

On the back of the mirror frame, make two marks with a pencil at 2 o'clock and 10 o'clock. At both marks, drill pilot holes for the eye screws; use a drill bit that is slightly smaller than the shaft of the eye screws. Twist in the eye screws, using the screwdriver for extra leverage if you need it.

6. Hang the mirror

Thread the decorative cord through the eye screws, and tie the ends together so the knot is behind the mirror. Hang the mirror. Adjust the knot as needed until the mirror is at the right height.

Style Note

For a jewel-like effect, string beads on the cord before you hang the mirror.

First-Timer Tip

If you share the bathroom with someone who is a lot taller or shorter, consider using an oval mirror instead.

Alternate Method

If you can't find studs to hang the board, you could install drywall anchors to hang it. But make sure that the space is free of plumbing pipes, which are often located in the hollow cavities between studs.

Drill the hole

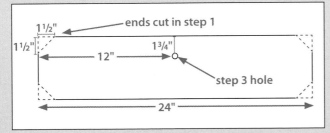

Mark the board 12 inches from one short edge and 1¾ inches from the top edge. There, drill a hole that's the same diameter as the machine screw all the way through the board.

$

Faux Roman shade

This simple-to-make window treatment looks like a Roman shade drawn halfway up, but it's actually sewn to cover just the top of the window. Light and airy, it's perfect for a bathroom overlooking a private backyard.

Materials

- decorator fabric, at least 4 inches wider than the window

- grosgrain ribbon, 1¼ inch wide and as long as the perimeter of the hemmed fabric plus 2 inches

- balsa wood, 1¼ inches by ¼ inch, cut ½ inch shorter than the shade width

Tools

- tape measure
- iron, and ironing pad or ironing board
- carpenter's square
- pencil
- yardstick
- scissors
- sewing pins
- thread
- sewing machine or needle
- double-sided mounting tape, 1 inch wide
- hammer
- nails, 1 inch to 1½ inches long

Style Notes

» The instructions here are for a tailored look. For a billowy look, don't iron the creases, and sew them down with only a few stitches at the side edges and middle.

» If you need more privacy, apply frosted contact paper or window film to the lower panes of glass.

▶ Steps

1. Measure

Measure the width and length you want for the shade. Add 4 inches to the width measurement, for side hems. Add 10 inches to the length measurement, allowing for a 1-inch double hem, three folds, and 1½ inches for mounting.

2. Cut

Iron the fabric. Close to one end, use the carpenter's square and pencil to mark a straight line across the fabric, perpendicular to an uncut edge. From the new line and the uncut edge, mark the length and width you need. Then, cut the fabric to those measurements. (If the fabric isn't wide enough for the width you need, cut two lengths and sew them together, matching the pattern.)

3. Hem

With the fabric wrong side up, turn up 1 inch on both sides. Then fold those over again (making double hems) to hide the cut edges. Iron, pin, and sew down the top folds to create hems. Do the same thing on the bottom of the fabric to create a lower hem.

Create the first fold

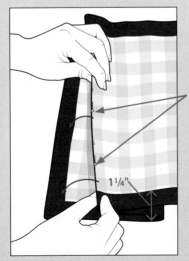

Place a line of pins 2½" from the hem edge. Pinch the line of pins into a fold and pull it down until it meets the hem edge.

1¼"

4. Add the trim

Cut two pieces of the grosgrain ribbon as long as the hemmed shade. Pin one piece to each side edge of the shade, on top of the side hems, then stitch along both edges of each ribbon. Cut two ribbons to match the shade width plus one inch. Turn under ½ inch at each end of both pieces. Pin, then stitch one piece along the bottom edge of the shade and the other 1½ inches below the top edge of the shade.

5. Create the first fold

Place the fabric right side up, with the bottom hem edge facing you. Place a line of pins 2½ inches up from the hem edge. Pinch the line of pins into a fold and pull it down until it meets the hem edge (see illustration). Flip back the upper fabric and iron the crease. Move the pins from the pin line and pin them through the front of the fabric to secure the crease. Place a few hand stitches every 3 inches along the crease (catching a few threads on the front of the fabric). Remove the pins as you go. Place another line of pins 2½ inches up from the new fold, and repeat the same process. Then, for the final fold, set the pins 3½ inches above the previous fold, and bring the pinched pleat down to only ¾ inch above the previous fold.

6. Assemble

Attach the mounting tape to the length of one side of the balsa wood. With the taped side of the wood facing up, align the top of the fabric with the top edge of the wood, and press the fabric down. Smooth the fabric as you press it against the tape. Flip the wood so the shade drapes over it, hiding the wood.

7. Attach

Hold the shade in position above the window. At one end of the balsa strip, maneuver the fabric out of the way and hammer a nail through the balsa and into the window frame or the wall (make sure you hit the wood framing). Repeat at the other side of the window. Then lift the shade and nail the rest of the balsa strip to the wall.

$ $

Mirror mosaic

Different-size glass tiles make this mirror fun and unique.

Materials

- ¾-inch plywood, cut to 56 inches by 32 inches

- wood shims

- three wood molding strips, ½ inch by 1¼ inch by 6 feet

- primer

- semi-gloss black latex paint

- 10 mirrors, 8 inches by 8 inches

- eight mirrors, 12 inches by 12 inches

- mirror adhesive

Tools

- pencil, yardstick, and utility knife

- handsaw and hammer

- wood glue and carpenter's level

- wire brads, ¾ inch

- sandpaper or sanding sponge, 100 grit

- finish nails, 1½ inch

- power drill (with bits) and screwdriver

- spacer blocks and drop cloth

- synthetic-bristle brush, 1 inch or 1½ inch

- caulk gun

- protective gloves (to handle glass)

- cleat picture hangers with fasteners (and toggle bolts if needed; see step 4)

- paint tray

▶Steps

1. Design the layout

With the pencil and the yardstick, draw the layout of the mirrors on the plywood base. You can follow the layout pictured here or design your own, but keep the edges even.

2. Create the angles

Place the shims on the plywood, side by side, to create angled supports for the mirrors (see illustration). Point the shims in each square in a single direction, but vary the direction from square to square. For instance: In one square, have the thick ends point up; in the next square, face them left. Shorten shims, where needed, with the handsaw, or score the wood with the utility knife and break off the excess. Use enough shims to completely cover the plywood. When all the shims are arranged, remove the shims in one square, apply glue to the backs, and put them back in place on the plywood, hammering in a couple of wire brads to secure them. Repeat for the remaining shims. Let dry.

3. Frame

With the handsaw, cut molding for the frame: two strips that are 56 inches long (for the sides) and two strips that are 33 inches long (for the top and bottom). Smooth the ends with the sandpaper or sanding sponge. Glue and nail the molding to the plywood with the narrow edge facing out. Attach the side strips first. Then attach the top and bottom strips. Let dry.

Create the angles

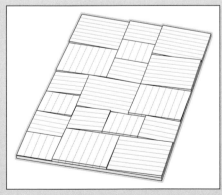

Place the shims on the plywood, side by side, to create angled supports for the mirrors. Point the shims in each square in a single direction, but vary the direction from square to square.

4. Attach the hangers

Locate studs within the wall. Using the drill, screwdriver, and carpenter's level, attach the cleat picture hangers to the studs and to the back of the plywood. If you can't find studs, use toggle bolts instead. (See pages 40–41 for how to find studs and install toggle bolts.)

5. Prime and paint

Place the whole frame on spacer blocks on the drop cloth. Pour some primer into the tray. With the brush, apply the primer to all the visible surfaces of the frame. It's okay if a little primer gets on the shims, but do not paint them because mirror adhesive bonds better to bare wood. Let dry. Apply the paint to the frame in the same way. When dry, brush on a second coat. Let dry.

6. Attach the mirrors and hang

Wearing the protective gloves to prevent getting cut, attach a corner mirror first. With the caulk gun, apply mirror adhesive to the shims or to the back of the mirror, following the instructions on the adhesive label. Place the mirror onto the shims and press down firmly enough to spread out the adhesive underneath. Repeat for the other mirrors. Then hang the mirror.

Style Note

If you want even more sparkle, start with mirror squares that have beveled edges, which allow each square to reflect light from five different angles.

First-Timer Tips

» Wood shims are typically about 8 inches long, but some stores also carry longer ones. Get some of each length, if possible, so you can support mirror tiles that are different sizes.

» Be sure to use adhesive labeled for use with mirrors, because other adhesives may contain ingredients that might corrode the mirror. Be certain that the adhesive is set before you hang the finished piece on the wall.

($)

Pipe toilet-paper holder

No need to fumble with a spring-loaded gizmo every time you want to install a new roll of toilet paper. This holder made of pipe fittings is easy and stylish.

Materials

- galvanized floor flange for ¾-inch-diameter pipe
- galvanized pipe nipple, ¾ inch by 2 inches
- galvanized 90-degree angle, ¾ inch
- galvanized pipe nipple, ¾ inch by 5 inches
- galvanized pipe cap, ¾ inch
- primer
- gloss or semi-gloss latex enamel

Tools

- drop cloth or newspaper
- paper towels and white vinegar
- scrap wood
- power drill (with bits) and screwdriver
- wood screws, 1 inch and 3 inch
- synthetic-bristle brush, 1 inch or 1½ inch
- screw-in anchors (if needed; see step 5)

Steps

1. Clean the parts

Place the pipe parts on the drop cloth or newspaper. To remove any oily deposits, thoroughly wipe each part with a paper towel moistened in white vinegar. Rinse with water. Let dry.

2. Assemble the parts

Screw the pipe parts together in the order they will lead out from the wall. Starting with the floor flange, screw on the 2-inch pipe nipple, then the 90-degree angle. Twist on the 5-inch nipple, then add the cap. Tighten everything as much as you can with hand pressure.

3. Prime and paint

To hold the tissue holder steady while you are painting it, temporarily attach it to the scrap wood using the drill, the screwdriver, and the shorter screws. Using the brush, apply the primer to all the surfaces, brushing away all drips as you go. Let dry. Then apply two coats of latex enamel. Let the paint dry after each coat.

4. Attach the holder

If there is an existing toilet-paper holder, remove it. Screw on the new holder using the same holes, if possible. If the holes don't line up, patch them (see page 28). To install a holder by making new holes, find a location where at least two of the screws will fasten to studs within the wall, and use the wall anchors to secure the other two screws. (See pages 40–41 for how to find studs and install wall anchors.) Slip on a roll of toilet paper.

First-Timer Tip

The pipe fittings may look sharp when they're unpainted, but don't leave them that way. The metal is coated with zinc, which, when unpainted, should be kept away from skin.

Alternate Method

For a different approach, spray-paint the holder instead of brushing on the paint. Apply a water-based primer first or the spray paint might peel.

Style Note

You can install the holder with the arm horizontal, or aimed straight up. Typical positioning is 26 inches above the floor and 8 to 12 inches forward of the toilet bowl.

($) ($)

Stone-framed mirror

Bring a bit of nature into your bathroom by framing a mirror with natural stone.

Materials

(not including mirror, ⅛–¼ inch thick)

- ¾-inch plywood, cut to 8 inches longer and wider than the mirror
- mesh-backed stone mosaic sheets
- mirror adhesive
- white polymer thin-set mortar
- penetrating sealer for stone
- pre-mixed tile grout

Tools

- drop cloth or newspaper
- pencil
- utility knife
- caulk gun
- plastic sheeting
- painter's masking tape, 1 inch or wider
- notched trowel
- foam brush and paper towels
- rubber gloves, bucket, sponge, and clean, dry cotton cloth
- power drill (with bits) and screwdriver
- screwdriver
- carpenter's level
- cleat picture hangers, with fasteners (and wall anchors if needed; see step 7)

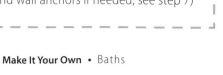

▶ Steps

1. Prep

Place the plywood on the drop cloth or newspaper. Center the mirror on the board and trace around the mirror with the pencil. Arrange the stone mosaic sheets around the mirror. Trim the sheets, if needed, by cutting the mesh with the utility knife. Set the trimmed sheets aside, maintaining the same orientation as when they were framing the mirror. Set the mirror aside.

2. Attach and cover the mirror

Cover the mirror with the plastic sheeting and tape the sheet firmly to the mirror's outside edges. With the caulk gun, apply mirror adhesive to the back of the mirror or to the plywood, as specified on the label, and press the mirror into place on the plywood. Let the adhesive cure.

3. Attach the stones

Using the notched trowel, spread the thin-set mortar around the mirror. Along each of the four sides of the mirror, hold the trowel at a slight angle as you spread the mortar from the mirror to the edge of the board, creating evenly high, parallel mortar ridges. Set the mosaic sheets straight down onto the mortar. Press the stones down firmly, but not so hard that you push all the mortar into gaps between the stones. Leave about 1/8 inch of mortar under the stones. Let dry.

4. Seal the stones

With the foam brush, coat the tops of the stones with the penetrating sealer. It's okay if some sealer drips down along the edges, but blot off any excess between the stones with a paper towel. Let dry.

5. Apply the grout

Complete this step and the next step outdoors, if possible. Wearing gloves, use your fingers to work the grout into the spaces around the stones. Then wipe across the stones with your gloved hand to remove most of the excess grout, leaving the tops of the stones about 1/4 inch above the grout. Also spread a thin film of grout along the outside edges of the frame. Check the grout label to see if you need to wait for the grout to stiffen before you clean the stones (step 6).

6. Clean the stones

Fill the bucket halfway with water. Dampen the sponge and wipe off the stones until they look relatively clean. Wash and wring out the sponge frequently as you go. Let the grout dry, following the instructions on the label. Finally, remove any remaining haze by rubbing the stones with a clean, dry cloth.

7. Hang the mirror

Locate studs within the wall. Using the drill, screwdriver, and carpenter's level, attach the cleat picture hangers to the studs and to the back of the framed mirror. If you can't find studs, use wall anchors instead. (See pages 40–41 for how to find studs and install wall anchors.) Remove the plastic from the mirror, and hang the frame.

Style Notes

》 Stone mosaic sheets come in different colors. For a vibrant look, choose stones that are red or even green. For additional flair, pry up a few of the stones and replace them with contrasting-colored stones or small pieces of sparkling glass.

》 For a shimmery look, use mosaic sheets covered with glass or ceramic tiles.

First-Timer Tips

》 Thin-set mortar remains sticky enough to adhere well to stone (or tile) for only about 10 minutes, so work in small sections when you are attaching the mosaics.

》 For best results, use a notched trowel that has the tooth pattern recommended for thin-set mortar.

($)

Hanging clipboards

For a bohemian look in the bathroom, hang clipboards that can hold everything from small artworks to your to-do list for the day.

Materials

- wooden or plastic clipboards
- clear or decorative contact paper (optional)
- cross-stitch or needlepoint mesh
- adhesive-backed magnetic tape

Tools

- pencil
- ruler
- scissors
- carpenter's level
- tape measure
- power drill with bits
- screws, 2½ inch or 3 inch
- screw-in wall anchors or molly bolts (if needed; see step 3)

Alternate Method

Instead of covering the clipboards with contact paper, brush on a couple of coats of clear acrylic, or brush on primer and then go wild with paint.

Steps

1. Cover the clipboards (optional)

This step is a good idea if you want to add water resistance to clipboards made of pressed wood fibers, or if you want to dress up your clipboards. Place a length of contact paper upside down on a work surface, and set one of the clipboards on top. With the pencil, trace around the bottom and most of the sides. Stop at the point on each side that corresponds to the bottom edge of the hardware. Use the ruler to draw a line across the contact paper between those two points to indicate where the top edge of the contact paper will be (you won't cover the clips). If the clipboard has rounded-over corners, draw a second outline ⅛ inch inside the first outline, and use this inside outline as your cutting guide. With the scissors, cut along the appropriate outline. Repeat for the other clipboards. Apply the contact paper to the front of each board.

2. Design the layout

Decide how high on the wall you want to hang each row of clipboards. To work out the horizontal spacing, set the clipboards on the floor and use the tape measure to make sure that the space between the clipboards is even. Mark the location of one clipboard hanger on the wall, then measure to the left and right and mark the remaining locations in that row, using the carpenter's level to make sure that the marks are horizontal. Mark any additional rows the same way.

3. Attach the hangers

With the drill and a bit that is a little smaller than the screws, drill into the wall at each location you marked. If the bit hits solid wood, screw in one of the screws there, leaving about ½ inch exposed to create a hanger. If the bit hits a hollow cavity, use a screw-in anchor or molly bolt. (See page 41 for how to install anchors.)

4. Hang and accessorize

Slip the clipboards onto the hangers and clip on postcard art or other items. If you want to store earrings, clip on a piece of cross-stitch or needlepoint mesh. To make daily to-do lists, clip on a stack of paper (and tape a pencil to a string, and tie that to the clipboard clip). Create a handy place for nail clippers and other metal toiletries, by applying strips of adhesive-backed magnetic tape.

Style Note
Vintage invoice holders (as pictured in the bottom row) work especially well for bathroom storage because you can loop scarves or belts through the wire clips on top.

Tiled backsplash

Protect your wall from splashes and give your bathroom a style boost by installing a mosaic tile backsplash.

Materials

- mesh-mounted mosaic tiles
- peel-and-stick tile setting mats (Bondera Tile Mat Set, SimpleMat Adhesive Tile Setting Mat)
- pre-mixed tile grout
- siliconized acrylic caulk for kitchen and bath, in squeeze tube

Tools

- rubber gloves, bucket, and sponge
- household cleaner
- drop cloth
- painter's masking tape, any width
- clean paper
- tape measure
- utility knife, with additional sharp blades
- pencil and ruler
- tile spacers
- grout float
- tile sponge
- clean, dry cloth
- caulk smoothing tool (optional)
- damp cloth

▶ Steps

1. Prep

If the mosaic sheets are dusty, wipe them with a damp sponge. Wearing gloves, wash the backsplash area and sink with water and the household cleaner. Let dry. Cover the sink and faucets with the drop cloth. Tape down the back edge.

2. Design the layout

Place the mosaic sheets side by side on clean paper on the floor. Measure the sink width, and decide whether you need to trim the mesh-mounted mosaics to fit this width. If so, cut through the mesh with the utility knife. With the pencil and the ruler, draw the outline of the tile on the wall. Mark the centerline on the wall and on the tile.

3. Apply the adhesive mats

With the utility knife, trim the adhesive mats to the sizes you need and press them to the part of the wall where the tiles will go, following the manufacturer's instructions.

4. Attach the tiles

Start with the sheet that includes the centerline you marked in step 2. Align that mark with the centerline on the wall. Use the tile spacers along the bottom edge to leave room for caulk (see step 7). Press the tiles firmly to the wall using the grout float. Apply the remaining sheets, working from the bottom up if you have more than one row.

5. Grout the tiles

Wearing gloves, use the grout float to work the grout into the spaces around the tiles. Use your fingers in tight spots. Wipe diagonally across the tiles to remove most of the excess grout. Spread a thin film of grout along the outside edges of the mosaics. Check the grout label to see if you need to wait for the grout to stiffen before you clean the tiles (see step 6).

6. Clean the tiles

Fill the bucket halfway with water. Dampen the tile sponge and wipe off the tiles until they look relatively clean; wash and wring out the sponge frequently as you go. Let the grout dry following the instructions on the label. Finally, remove any remaining haze by rubbing the tiles with a clean, dry cloth.

7. Caulk

With the utility knife, cut the tip of the caulk tube at a 45-degree angle. Apply a bead of caulk between the tile and the sink. Smooth it with the smoothing tool or a damp finger. Immediately wipe away the excess with a damp cloth. Remove the drop cloth. Let the caulk dry.

Alternate Method

Some adhesive mats don't work with certain types of tile, such as glass or slate. If you can't use mats, switch to premixed tile mastic and spread it with a notched trowel. You'll need to wait at least a day before you add the grout.

First-Timer Tip

If you can't trim the mosaics to the exact width of the sink, leave the sheets a little wider than you need. Then extend the mosaics past the sink equally on both sides.

Style Note

To complement your new backsplash, find another surface in the bathroom that can be tiled with the same mosaic design, such as the top of a step stool or a shelf where you could display plants.

6

Stencils and artful touches

Not everything in a bathroom needs to be functional. Some elements are just for fun and style. In this chapter, you'll find projects that both inspire and delight. Use stencils to create intricate designs on your vanity cabinet or tub. Hang colorful fabric pennants across the room. Frame a set of small mirrors on the wall, or paint a bold design on your toilet seat cover. With our detailed instructions and a little imagination, anything becomes possible.

3-D Wall Art ⌄

Artwork hung over the tub can have a great impact and offer stylish reflections to boot. For instance, these metallic flowers add depth to the wall. Add a reflective table to match, and suddenly your bathroom doubles as a modern art gallery.

Mirror, Mirror ⌃

Adding art to your bathroom can be as easy as painting a pretty border around your mirror. Complement your design by bringing matching elements into the room, such as the starfish perched on the sink that's pictured here.

≪ Think Pink!

For a soft, whimsical look, paint the bathroom white and use pink as an accent color for different accessories in the room. Light blue and yellow accents would offer a similar effect.

Creative Lighting »

Artful light fixtures can do wonders for a room. Instead of using ordinary overhead lights, hang alternate light sources, like pendants in star or diamond shapes. For beauty and practicality, let them frame the mirror.

Memory Lane Photos »

Do you have a box filled with old black-and-white photos of family members from prior generations? Scan, print, and frame copies of the photos and display them in a room that everyone visits—the bathroom.

Stenciled Seascape »

A tub can take up a lot of real estate in a bathroom—why not make yours a central design piece? With a simple stencil, you can paint a small school of fish on your tub exterior. See page 148 for complete tub-stenciling instructions.

($) ($) ($)

Fabric pennants

As a simple decoration, flying pennants add quick color and a breezy cheerfulness to your bathroom.

Materials

- two eye screws that the cord fits through (if needed; see step 1)
- two screw-in drywall anchors (if needed; see step 1)
- sash cord or other slender rope
- brightly colored fabric

Tools

- power drill with bits (if needed to install eye screws; see step 1)
- screwdriver (if needed to install eye screws; see step 1)
- scrap paper
- ruler and pencil
- pinking shears or scissors
- transparent tape
- sewing pins
- sewing machine or needle
- thread and scissors

Maintenance Tip

If you don't have pinking shears, rub a little liquid seam sealer along any edges that were cut with standard scissors to keep flags from fraying over time.

Steps

1. Choose or create supports

If you have curtain rods, a shower rod, or other high features that you can wrap a cord around, you can attach the ends of your flag cord there. Otherwise, attach your cord to the wall using eye screws. If you're fastening to wood panels or studs in the wall (see page 40 for how to find studs), drill holes slightly smaller than the eye-screw shaft. If you're fastening to a hollow wall, use screw-in wall anchors sized to the eye-screw shaft. Then, install the eye screws.

2. Design the flags

Cut your flags out on scrap paper. A pleasing size is 12 inches long and 8 inches wide, but you can experiment with different sizes. To create even triangles, fold the paper in half lengthwise and draw a straight line that starts at the fold on one end and angles out to the edges at the other. Cut along the line, through both layers. Unfold the paper triangles and tape them to the cord to see how they look.

3. Make the pattern

When you have your dimensions, draw the shape you want on scrap paper. To allow for a hem where you can string the cord, add a band 1½ inches deep along the wide end of the triangle. Square the ends of the band, making it only as long as the wide end of the triangle.

4. Cut the fabric

Pin the pattern to one piece of fabric. With pinking shears, cut along its edges. To cut the maximum number of pennants from a single width of fabric, cut flags side by side, alternating the direction of the tip.

5. Sew

Leaving some cord free on one end, wrap the hem allowance of the first flag around the cord one full turn, so no raw edge is exposed. Pin through the flag to secure it to the cord. Stitch through the flag and the cord all along the hem. Sew on the remaining flags, leaving even spacing and some flag-free cord at the other end. Use the flag-free ends to tie up the cord.

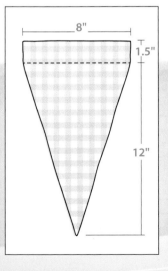

Style Note

Flags generally look best if they are longer than they are wide.

8"

1.5"

12"

Style Note

For an interesting mix of colors and patterns, visit a quilting store and buy different patterns in "fat quarters" (fabric pieces 18 inches by 22 inches) and "fat eights" (11 inches by 18 inches).

($) ($) ($)

Stenciled bath cabinet

Cotton swabs, medicine bottles, make-up—the bathroom cabinet isn't exactly the most exciting thing to look at. That is, until you make it over with painted-on stencils in an inside-out color scheme. Now, looking for a nail file becomes a whole lot more fun.

Materials

(not including materials for prepping, priming, and painting base coats)

- gloss or semi-gloss latex paint or enamel (two vividly contrasting colors)
- stencil with a dotted spiral or other all-over, repeating design
- repositionable spray adhesive

Tools

- scrap paper
- shallow container for paint
- stencil brush
- damp rag
- tape measure
- painter's masking tape, any width

Steps

1. Prep, prime, and paint

Follow the procedures on page 59 to prep, prime, and paint the interior and exterior of the cabinet. Paint the interior of the cabinet with the color you'll use for the stenciled design on the front, and vice versa.

2. Create the design

Place a sheet of scrap paper under the stencil, and choose some elements from the stencil for the first part of your design. Pour a little paint into a shallow container, such as a discarded saucer or a large jar lid. Dab the tips of the bristles of the stencil brush into the paint, and blot them on a different piece of paper to remove excess paint. Paint that section of the stencil, dabbing the brush in and out rather than painting sideways. Continue painting adjoining sections until you have enough pieces for the overall design.

3. Affix the design

With the tape measure, determine the height and width of the cabinet front. Mark the same dimensions on a flat surface, such as a tabletop. Arrange the sample sheets there in your design. Then use the painter's masking tape to affix them, sheet by sheet, to the cabinet front in the same arrangement.

4. Stencil the cabinet front

Remove one sample sheet, and tape up the stencil in its place, aligned to re-create that part of the design. Or, spray the back of the stencil with repositionable spray adhesive first and press the stencil to the cabinet. Paint that section of the stencil, using the technique you practiced in step 2. Always start at the edges of a cutout and paint toward the center. After you complete the section, remove the stencil and clean the back with the damp rag. Take down another sample sheet, not adjacent to where you just painted, reposition the stencil, and paint that section. Repeat until you complete the design. You may need to pause periodically for the paint to dry on adjoining sections.

5. Stencil the cabinet back

Stencil the back wall of the cabinet in the same way, using the contrasting paint color.

Style Note

Geometric patterns work well with this inside-out effect, but so do themed designs. For example, with a leaf stencil, you might want spring green leaves on the exterior and fall colors inside.

Maintenance Tip

If your cabinet is used a lot, brush a coat of matte acrylic over the completed stencil, especially on the exterior, after the paint fully dries.

($)

Stencil-art roller shades

Blank white roller shades let in a lot of light, but they can also be a bit, well, blank. Add a little excitement to your shades by stenciling designs on them. It's easy and inexpensive—and your shades will be total originals.

Materials

(not including the fabric roller shades)

- printed image to copy (optional)
- stencil board or heavy card stock
- screen printing ink or fabric paint suitable for shade material

Tools

- photocopier
- glue stick
- cutting board, at least half the size of your image
- craft knife with extra blades
- drop cloth
- tape measure
- masking tape, any width, or repositionable spray adhesive
- stencil brush

Steps

1. Prep the image

Select an image from a clip-art book or website, or draw one yourself. With a photocopier, enlarge the image to the desired size, if necessary. For a larger image than your photocopier can handle, enlarge each half separately.

2. Create your stencil

With the glue stick, coat the back of the photocopy. Make sure to spread the glue onto all areas. Flip the image and adhere it to the stencil board or card stock. (If you enlarged halves of the image separately, glue each half to the board.) Let the glue dry. Then lay the stencil board on the cutting board. With the craft knife, carefully cut out the image. You may need to go over your cuts more than once to be able to lift out the image. Be sure to use sharp blades to avoid ragged edges; replace the blades as needed.

3. Position the stencil

Position one roller shade flat on the drop cloth with the room side facing up. Place the stencil on the shade. Use the tape measure to make sure the stencil is centered. Adhere the stencil (or multiple stencil sections) to the shade with masking tape or by spraying the back of the stencil with repositionable spray adhesive.

4. Paint

With the stencil brush, dab the printing ink or fabric paint through the stencil cutouts onto the shade. To keep the stencil tight against the shade (to prevent the ink or paint from seeping), press your fingers down on the stencil near the section you're painting. Let dry.

5. Set and hang

Remove the stencil and follow any paint label instructions for setting the color. Repeat on any additional shades. Hang as you would any roller shades.

Style Note

To reverse the image for a second shade, as shown here, flip the stencil over. (Be sure that the ink or paint on the stencil board is completely dry before you flip over the stencil.)

First-Timer Tips

» When selecting an image, choose a silhouette without intricate details so that the stencil is easier to cut and use. And choose an image with design elements that don't overlap, so you can cut the pattern out as one piece.

» Screen printing ink works only on absorbent fabric. Test the fabric's absorbency by sprinkling on a little water. If the water beads up, the ink won't work on that fabric.

($) ($)

Framed mirrors

Tie a collection of secondhand frames together by painting them all one color palette, installing mirrors in them, and then arranging them above the sink for an ultrachic effect.

Materials

(not including sturdy wood frames with edge clips)

- two or three colors of latex paint, sample sizes
- mirror glass, ⅛ inch thick, cut to fit frames

Tools

- sandpaper or sanding sponge, 180 grit
- microfiber dust cloth
- drop cloth or newspaper
- scraps of wood (to support frames while paint dries)
- synthetic-bristle brush, 1 inch or 1½ inch
- painter's masking tape (if using two colors on any of the frames)
- hammer
- picture hangers or nails

Steps

1. Design the layout

Arrange the frames on the floor or a worktable in the same way you'd like them on the wall. Decide which color (or colors) to paint each frame.

2. Prep

Remove any mats and glass from the frames. Lightly sand any sheen off the wood with the sandpaper or sanding sponge. Wipe all the surfaces with the dust cloth.

3. Paint

Position the drop cloth or newspaper, and arrange the wood scraps to support the frames. With the synthetic-bristle brush, paint each frame a different color, taking care to avoid leaving drips in corners. For frames that will have a contrasting band of color (as in the largest mirror pictured here), paint the entire frame the main color now. After the first coat of paint is dry, apply painter's masking tape to any frame where you want a contrasting band. Affix the tape along both sides of the band. Press the tape down firmly on the edges facing the band. Brush on the second color. Let dry, and remove the tape.

4. Install the mirrors

Take the frames to a glass shop and buy custom-cut mirrors for them. The mirrors should be thin enough to fit the recesses in the frames. Place the mirrors in the frames, and secure the edge clips or other devices for holding the frame and its contents together.

5. Mount the mirrors

With the hammer, tap the picture hangers or nails into the wall and then hang the framed mirrors. (If the walls are plaster, drill small holes for the hangers or nails before you tap them in so you don't crack the plaster.)

First-Timer Tip

To see how the layout looks on the wall before you hang the mirrors, cut out pieces of paper in the same sizes as the frames and affix them to the wall with tape.

Style Notes

» For a uniform palette, use a single basic paint color, but create different tints by adding various amounts of white to the basic color.

» When you're arranging frames that are different styles and shapes, experiment with an asymmetrical arrangement, as shown here.

($) ($)

Photo wall

For the ultimate in DIY bathroom decor, hang a waterproof photo display above your tub or sink.

Materials
- tempered hardboard, 1/8 inch thick
- clear acrylic sheet
- primer
- black latex paint, any sheen
- photographs

Tools
- tape measure
- yardstick
- pencil
- jigsaw or circular saw
- sandpaper or sanding sponge, 100 grit
- microfiber dust cloth
- fine-tip marker
- utility knife
- drop cloth or newspaper
- paint tray
- roller, 9 inch or mini
- double-sided tape, any width
- black plastic tape, 1½ inch
- double-coated mounting tape, any width

Steps

1. Cut the hardboard
Determine how big you want your photo wall, and use the tape measure, yardstick, and pencil to mark the length and width on the hardboard. With the jigsaw or circular saw, cut just outside the lines. Smooth the cut edges with the sandpaper or sanding sponge, and wipe the surface with the dust cloth.

2. Cut the acrylic sheet
Mark the acrylic sheet for the same length and width using the fine-tip marker. To make the first cut, trace against the yardstick with the utility knife. Go over the line several times until you have scored about halfway through the sheet. Then place the acrylic sheet so that the score line lies over the edge of a table. Push down sharply on the overhanging acrylic sheet, snapping it along the line. Trim the rest of the sheet the same way.

3. Prime and paint the hardboard
Set the hardboard on the drop cloth or newspaper, smooth side up. Pour some primer into the paint tray, and use the roller to apply an even coat to the hardboard. Let dry. Then apply the latex paint in the same way. Let dry.

4. Arrange and attach the photos
Arrange the photos on the painted hardboard, leaving at least ¾ inch free around the edges. Then, remove one photo, apply double-sided tape to the reverse side, and press the photo back into place. Repeat for the remaining photos.

5. Cover and apply the edging
Position the hardboard with the photos so that one side overhangs the edge of the work surface by several inches. Place the acrylic sheet over the photos, and align the edges. Create a frame for the photo display by applying the black plastic tape along the outermost ½ inch of the display. Apply the tape over the acrylic sheet, wrapping the excess tape around the back of the hardboard. Press the tape down firmly on both sides.

6. Install
Apply double-coated mounting tape to the back of the hardboard. Press the panel to the wall.

Alternate Methods

» If you want to be able to change the photo display, use adhesive-backed hook-and-loop tape instead of the black plastic tape. This is not a waterproof option so position the board away from any wet surfaces.

» For a simpler project, make a smaller display. Use hardboard and an acrylic sheet in a stock size, such as 2 feet by 4 feet.

($) ($)

Stenciled tub

Claw-foot tubs give any bathroom a vintage feel. Add a special touch by stenciling on a delicate design.

Materials

- stencil with a floral or other all-over, repeating design
- gloss or semi-gloss latex paint or enamel, sample size
- repositionable spray adhesive

Tools

- rubber gloves, bucket, and sponge
- household cleaner
- tape measure
- pencil
- scrap paper
- shallow container for paint
- stencil brush
- damp rag
- artist's brush and base-color paint, or a cotton swab and rubbing alcohol (see step 5 for details)

Style Note

To give your bathroom a coordinated look, choose a stencil color that matches your towels and bath mat.

Steps

1. Prep

Wearing gloves, wash the tub exterior with water and the cleaner. Let dry. (It's not necessary to repaint the tub first, but if you want to, follow the procedures on page 68.)

2. Design the layout

Measure the length of the tub along the front of the exterior, and determine the midpoint. Mark that point in pencil. Using the stencil as a guide, lightly mark off stencil-wide increments to the left and right of the midpoint. Then repeat this process, but start with the stencil centered over the midpoint instead of alongside it. Decide which arrangement will result in a more balanced look. Also decide how far down from the rim you want the stencil. Hold the stencil in the first position. Using the pencil, mark the tub through the registration marks (small openings on the stencil). Repeat for the remaining positions. Make sure that all the top marks are an equal distance from the rim.

3. Practice

Place a sheet of scrap paper under the stencil, and pour a little paint into a shallow container. Dab the tips of the bristles of the stencil brush into the paint. Blot them on a different piece of paper to remove excess paint, then practice painting the stencil. Dab the brush in and out, rather than painting sideways. Always start at the edges of a cutout and paint toward the center. Apply a very thin but uniform layer of paint in all openings, taking care to avoid smearing the edges. Clean the stencil with a damp rag.

4. Stencil the tub

Spray the back of the stencil with repositionable spray adhesive. Line up the stencil with the marks you drew in step 2, and press the stencil to the tub. Paint the first design, then remove the stencil and clean the back. Let the first design dry. Then reposition the stencil. Repeat until you complete the design.

5. Touch up

If you painted the tub recently, use the artist's brush to dab a little of the tub color over the pencil marks from step 2. Otherwise, erase the marks by dabbing on a little rubbing alcohol with a cotton swab. Be gentle so that you don't rub off the paint.

First-Timer Tip
Stencil paint should be dabbed on thinly so that it dries almost instantly. To test your technique, rub a finger over the samples you make in step 3 a minute or so after you paint them. If any paint comes off on your finger, try again with less paint.

Ⓢ

Colorfully framed photos

Create a unique photo display in your bathroom by collecting some mismatched secondhand picture frames and painting them with a carefully orchestrated palette.

Materials

- wooden picture frames with glass
- black-and-white photographs or other artwork
- three to five colors of latex paint, sample sizes
- precut mats, if needed

Tools

- sandpaper or sanding sponge, 180 grit
- microfiber dust cloth
- drop cloth or newspaper
- scraps of wood
- synthetic-bristle brush, 1 inch or 1½ inch
- hammer
- picture hangers or nails

Steps

1. Design the layout

Choose which of your photographs to pair with each frame, determine their arrangement on the wall, and select which color to use for each.

2. Prep

Remove the mat and glass from each frame. Lightly sand any sheen off the wood with the sandpaper or sanding sponge. Remove any residue with the dust cloth.

3. Paint

Position the drop cloth or newspaper, and arrange the wood scraps to support the frames. With the brush, paint the frames different colors, taking care to avoid leaving drips in the corners.

4. Mat

When the frames are dry, take them to a framing shop and buy precut mats for them, all in the same color. Or reuse any mats of the same color that you already have. If you have an odd-size frame and can't find a precut mat that fits, choose a photograph that doesn't need a mat for that frame.

5. Mount

Assemble the mats and photographs in the frames. Using the hammer, tap the picture hangers or nails into the wall and then hang the framed pictures. (If the walls are plaster, drill small holes for the hangers or nails before you tap them in so you don't crack the plaster.)

Style Note

When choosing paint colors, look for multicolor paint chips supplied by many paint manufacturers. All the colors on each chip usually go together well.

$

Painted toilet seat

For a completely original look, paint the seat and lid a bright new color, and then stencil a star on the lid.

Materials

(not including toilet seat or lid)

- primer (use plastic primer if the toilet seat is plastic)
- semi-gloss latex paint (for base color), 1 quart
- matte or gloss latex paint (for accent color), sample size

Tools

- screwdriver
- adjustable wrench
- spacer blocks
- drop cloth or newspaper
- rubber gloves, bucket, and sponge
- household cleaner
- sandpaper or sanding sponge, 180 grit
- microfiber dust cloth
- synthetic-bristle brush, 1½ inch or 2 inch
- pencil and ruler
- scrap paper, 8½ inches by 11 inches
- protractor
- scissors
- painter's masking tape, any width
- artist's brush

Steps

1. Prep the lid and seat

Remove the lid and seat with the screwdriver and wrench. Position the spacer blocks on the drop cloth or newspaper, and place the lid and seat on top of the blocks. Wearing gloves, wash both parts with water and the cleaner. Let dry. If the parts are wood, scuff-sand all the surfaces with the sandpaper or sanding sponge. Wipe the surfaces with the dust cloth.

2. Prime and paint the lid and seat

Use the synthetic-bristle brush to apply primer to the top and outside edges of the seat and lid, brushing around the lower edges to smooth out any drips. Let dry. Flip over the parts and paint the backs. Let dry. Apply the base paint in the same way. When the paint is dry, add a second coat. Let dry.

3. Design the star

With the ruler and pencil, make a mark in the center of the scrap paper. For an 8-inch star, as pictured here, use the pencil and ruler to draw a 4-inch line up from the center to the first star point. Place the protractor's center over the paper's center point, and line up the protractor base line with the line you just drew. Make a mark at 72 degrees. Draw another 4-inch line from the center through the new mark and out to the end of the next point. Using each new line as the next base line, draw three more equally spaced lines radiating from the center. Then draw lines connecting the outside end of each line with the outside ends of the line farthest away. Cut out the star with the scissors.

4. Paint the star

Tape the star to the center of the toilet seat lid. Then apply the masking tape carefully along the edges of the star, creating a clean outline. Remove the paper star, and press down the tape edges facing the star shape that is left in the center of the lid. Using the synthetic-bristle brush, apply the contrasting paint within the taped-off area, brushing from the tape toward the center of the star. When the paint is dry, brush on a second coat. Let dry.

5. Complete

Remove the tape. With the artist's brush, fill in any gaps in the design. Reattach the seat and lid.

First-Timer Tip

If the screws or nuts are corroded and you can't easily remove the lid and seat, paint them in place. Drape a plastic drop cloth over the ceramic parts of the toilet, then cover the hardware with painter's masking tape.

Alternate Method

If you are painting a plastic toilet seat, use special spray paint formulated to work on plastic for the base coat. With this kind of spray paint, you can often skip scuff-sanding and priming (check the label to be sure).

Style Note

Use your protractor (as instructed in step 3) to create an elegant 8-inch star.

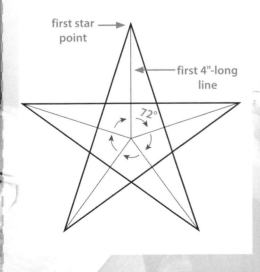

first star point

first 4"-long line

72°

Resource Guide

The following list includes organizations, manufacturers, and retail sources that you might find helpful as you undertake projects to spruce up your bathroom.

Organizations and Associations

For most organizations, type "bathroom" into the website's search box to find pertinent information.

ADA Standards for Accessible Design
http://www.ada.gov/stdspdf.htm

American Institute of Architects
www.aia.org

American Society of Interior Designers
www.asid.org

Energy Star
www.energystar.gov
A government program that lists energy-efficient products, including bathroom ventilating fans

International Code Council
http://www.iccsafe.org
An organization that develops building codes used by many communities

National Kitchen & Bath Association
www.nkba.org

WaterSense
www.epa.gov/watersense
A program that identifies high-efficiency toilets, faucets, showerheads, and other products; also lists rebates

Design Inspiration

Apartment Therapy
www.apartmenttherapy.com

Design*Sponge
www.designsponge.com

Houzz
www.houzz.com

Pinterest
www.pinterest.com

Project Materials

Bondera Tile Mat Set
www.bonderatilematset.com
Tile setting mat for "Tiled backsplash," page 130

Bosch Glass & Tile Bit
www.boschtools.com
Tile-cutting bit for "Shower hooks," page 110

eBay
www.ebay.com
Vintage storage units and furniture to repurpose

Ferm Living Shop
www.fermlivingshop.com
Uncoated wallpaper, including by the yard

FrogTape Painter's Tape
www.frogtape.com
Edge-blocking tape, mentioned on page 30

Henny Donovan Motif
www.hennydonovanmotif.co.uk
Dotty spiral stencil for "Stenciled bath cabinet," page 140

Home Depot
www.homedepot.com
Home center with tile, paint, plumbing parts, wood for projects

Hygge and West
www.hyggeandwestshop.com
Wallpaper by the yard, in clearance section

Knobs and Hardware
www.knobsandhardware.com
Shelf brackets for "Bracket shelf with hooks," page 84

Lee Valley Tools
www.leevalley.com
Hooks, brackets, and specialty hardware

Lowe's
www.lowes.com
Home center with tile, paint, plumbing parts, wood for projects

Royal Design Studio
www.royaldesignstudio.com
Pattern stencils for "Stenciled tub," page 148

SimpleMat
http://thesimplemat.com
Tile setting mat for "Tiled backsplash," page 130

Smith Woodworks & Design Inc.
www.niceknobs.com
Wooden knobs for "Wood knob towel hooks," page 114

The Stencil Library
www.stencil-library.com

TAP Plastics
www.tapplastics.com
Fiberglass rod for "Cabinet with curtain," page 92, and acrylic sheet for "Photo wall," page 146

Versatex Screen Printing Ink
www.jacquardproducts.com
Screen printing ink for "Stencil-art roller shades," page 142

Zinsser
www.rustoleum.com
Shellac-based primer for "Painted tub," page 68

Credits

Photography

ACP/Marie Helene Clauzon/trunk archive.com: 126; ACP/Sue Ferris/trunkarchive.com: 12; ACP/Maree Homer/trunkarchive.com: 66; ACP/Chris Warnes/trunkarchive.com: 85; Lucas Allen/GMA Images: 29 (Design: Alexandra Angle), 72 (Design: Alexandra Angle); Serge Anton/Living Inside: 42, 98, 115, back cover left; Jan Baldwin/Narratives: 55; Kira Brandt/Living Inside: 108 right (Stylist: Ulrikke Gercke); Adrian Briscoe/IPC+ Syndication: 3 middle, 104–105, 120; Rob D. Brodman: 151; Alun Callender/Narratives: 47; Jennifer Cheung/Botanica/Getty Images: 9 top left; Lisa Cohen/Taverne Agency: 108 left; Jonn Coolidge: 8 top; Jeffery Cross: 18, 31; GAP Interiors/Graham Atkins-Hughes: 17; GAP Interiors/Bill Kingston: 135 right; James Gardiner/IPC+ Syndication: 149; William Geddes: 2 middle (Stylist: Marcus Hay), 20–21 (Stylist: Marcus Hay); William Geddes/Beateworks/Corbis: 54 left (Design: Sterling Baths); David Gilles/IPC+ Syndication: 93; Tria Giovan: 37 (Design: Heather Chadduck), 43; Stewart Grant/Photoshot/Red Cover: 6–7, 9 top right; Art Gray: 71; Raimund Koch/GMA Images: 62 (Design: Adib Cure and Carie Penabad); Nathalie Krag/Taverne Agency: 88; Chuck Kuhn: 32, 45; Ericka McConnell: 81 left (Styling: Philippine Scali); Ellen McDermott: 11 (Interior design: Anthony-Wright Interiors), 59 (Interior design: Anthony-Wright Interiors); James Merrell/IPC+ Syndication: 141, back cover center; A. Mezza & E. Escalante/Narratives: 54 right; Ngoc Minh Ngo/Taverne Agency: 109, 122, 129, 145, 156; Laura Moss: 2 right (Builder: New World Home), 19 (Interior design: Jamie Herzlinger), 33, 48, 50–51 (Builder: New World Home), 61 (Builder: New World Home); Photoshot/Red Cover/Nina Assam: 65; Photoshot/Red Cover/Steve Back: 9 bottom right; Photoshot/Red Cover/Steve Dalton: 80; Photoshot/Red Cover/Christopher Drake: 107 right; Photoshot/Red Cover/Victoria Gomez: 111; Photoshot/Red Cover/Stewart Grant: 2 left, 94, 134; Photoshot/Red Cover/Winfried Heinze: 44; Photoshot/Red Cover/Di Lewis: 136 right; Photoshot/Red Cover/Jean Maurice: 53 top left; Photoshot/Red Cover/Paul Ryan-Goff: 53 right; Photoshot/Red Cover/Henry Wilson: 147; Photoshot/Red Cover/Mel Yates: 4–5; Laura Resen: 23; Laura Resen/Art Rep Team: 40; Lisa Romerein: 154; Mark Roskams/GMA Images: 74 (Design: Gene Meyer), 135 top left (Design: Gene Meyer); Eric Roth: 26, 82 left, 97 (Design: Susan Sargent Designs), 116, 118; Alexandra Rowley, courtesy of Faucher Artists: 77; Jeremy Samuelson: 106; Robert Sanderson/IPC+ Syndication: 112, back cover right; Robert Sanderson/Narratives: 107 top left; Sarramon-Cardinale/Photononstop/Jupiterimages: 136 left; Annie Schlechter: 3 left, 52 (Design: Sasha Adler), 78–79, 91; Annie Schlechter/GMA Images: 83 (Design: Nathalie Smith); Alan Shortall/Corner House Stock Photo: 82 right; Thomas J. Story: 3 right, 9 bottom left (Stylist: Miranda Jones), 15, 16 (Design: Francesca Quagliata), 24 (Design: Levy Art & Architecture), 34, 132–133, 143 both, 151 inset; Tim Street-Porter: 8 bottom, 69 (Design: Joseph Giovannini); Lucinda Symons/Country Homes & Interiors/IPC+ Syndication: 101; Chris Tubbs/Gap Interiors: 139; Mikkel Vang/Taverne Agency: 158; Bjorn Wallander: Front cover (Art direction: Philippine Scali; Stylist: Ethel Brennan; Fabric for shades from Hable Construction), 1 (Art direction: Philippine Scali; Stylist: Ethel Brennan), 57 (Art direction: Philippine Scali; Stylist: Ethel Brennan; Fabric for shades from Hable Construction), 102 (Art direction: Philippine Scali, Stylist: Ethel Brennan), 125 (Art direction: Philippine Scali; Stylist: Ethel Brennan), 153 (Art direction: Philippine Scali; Stylist: Ethel Brennan); Melissa Warner: 38–39 (Design: Melissa Warner, Massucco Warner Miller Interior Design); Simon Whitmore/IPC+ Syndication: 13, 81 right, 130; Tim Young/IPC+ Syndication: 137; Hans Zeegers/Taverne Agency: 86.

Illustration

Beverley Bozarth Colgan: 22 (all); Haisam Hussein: 67 (both), 89, 95, 96 (all), 99 (both), 103, 113, 121, 123, 139; Margaret Sloan: 87 (both), 119, 153

Special Thanks

Jess Chamberlain, Erika Ehmsen, Mark Hawkins, Miranda Jones, Charla Lawhon, Megan Lee, Laura Martin, Haley Minick, Marie Pence, Alan Phinney, Lorraine Reno, Margaret Sloan, Katie Tamony, Angela Tolosa

Index